HENRY MOORE

HENRY MOORE

BY JOHN RUSSELL

G. P. Putnam's Sons, New York

Copyright © John Russell, 1968

Library of Congress Catalog Card Number:
LCC 68–31740

First published in Great Britain by Allen Lane
The Penguin Press, Vigo Street, London W1

First published in the United States in 1968
by G. P. Putnam's Sons, 200 Madison Avenue,
New York, N.Y. 10016

Designed by Germano Facetti

Endpaper and Frontispiece photographs from *Private
View* by kind permission of Lord Snowdon

Made and printed in Great Britain by Jarrold & Sons
Ltd, Norwich

This book owes a great deal to the kindness and
friendly co-operation of Henry Moore, both in
answering innumerable questions and in giving me
the freedom of his photographic archive. Where he
is quoted verbatim, the quotations come in many
cases from tape-recordings of interviews with Vera
Lindsay and myself which were commissioned by
the *Sunday Times*. Other quotations come from
Henry Moore on Sculpture, an anthology edited by
Philip James and published by Macdonald.

I should also like to acknowledge the hard and
patient work put in by Mr Moore's secretary, Mrs
Betty Tinsley, and the encouragement which I
received from Mr H. R. Fischer and Mr James
Kirkman of Marlborough Fine Art, London.

I have also had the good fortune, not for the
first time, of working on the production side with
Germano Facetti, whose enthusiasm, perseverance
and fine judgement made a continuous pleasure
out of what is usually esteemed to be drudgery.

J.R.

To Margaret Scolari Barr

I

In the career of Henry Moore, legend must from the start be disentangled from fact.

How often, for instance, do we not read in exhibition catalogues that Moore was 'born on 30 July 1898, the son of a miner'? The date is incontrovertible: but 'the son of a miner' causes many people to picture for themselves a self-made genius with Lawrentian overtones, an unlettered giant powered by imperious instinct and ill at ease in the world of ideas. For that matter, Moore's open and easy address and unaffected habits of speech are in many ways misleading. Only on closer acquaintance is it apparent that he systematically underplays his own stature as a man who for half a century has kept in touch with the things that matter in many departments of human activity.

This was an inherited capacity. His father was not 'a miner', in the conventional sense of the word, but a thoughtful and tenacious individual who would have gone quickly to the top if he had had a chance of formal education. Nearer to H. G. Wells than to D. H. Lawrence in his orientation, he set great store by brains, and by the proper use of them. He had pulled himself out of the pits by mastering, unaided, the mathematical and technical knowledge which were needed to become a mining engineer. Three of his eight children became teachers, and when Henry was a boy his father gave him just the guidance which he needed. Both his parents set, in fact, an example of sustained conscientious exertion: his father in the grinding disciplines of self-help, and his mother in the continuous hard labour of raising eight children. 'She had tremendous physical stamina. She used to work from morning till night until she was over seventy. To be a sculptor, you have to have that sort of energy and that sort of stamina. Sculpture is of all the fine arts the one in which you have to have an absolute physical fitness. You can't – in the early stages at least – be tired or ill if you want to be a sculptor.'

Moore was the seventh of eight children. When he was twelve or thirteen his younger sister died and he had, more than ever, the privileges of the youngest child in a large and well-knit family. 'There's no doubt that I had a very good time at home and took for granted the warmth and friendship and happiness of a large family.' When Moore speaks of his childhood he describes, above all, a situation. There is little of the atmospheric or anecdotal

2 Bird and Egg *Cumberland alabaster length 22 in.* 1934
Artist's Collection

detail with which many people lard their first memories: what comes over is the sense of being at home in a manageable society. And, whereas the classic English childhood of the sensitive person is made up of distances suddenly beyond measurement, misjudgements of capacity, and social illusions which burst open and leave permanent wounds behind them, Moore progressed from stage to stage in orderly style. If he had extravagant ambitions, his father knew better than to damp them; and his schools were of the kind in which teachers took time out to foster an exceptional boy. If there were traumatic incidents, no one knows of them. If we compare the boyhood of Matthew Smith, for instance, who came from what could be called a more privileged milieu, we can only wonder at the maturing of great gifts which came, in the one case, from sustained agony of the nerves and spirit, and in the other from what now seems like an almost Biblical simplicity of life and an earnest, regular, high-souled will to succeed. It came naturally to Moore to be at one with his environment, and

he was further helped in this by the teachers whom he still names with gratitude and affection: T.R.Dawes, the headmaster of the local grammar school, and Miss Gostick the art mistress, and one or two others who put it about that there was more to education than passing examinations. Moore believes that 'Such people are there all the time, for everybody, if any one wants to find them.' But in the teacher/pupil relationship something was changed forever, surely, when radio and cinema and television broke into what had been a closed circuit between one mind and another. In terms of 'facilities' the years immediately before 1914 may now look almost medieval; but in human terms education still reached out beyond the medieval and had as its highest achievement something near to the Socratic ideal of teaching. And Moore was one of those who profited most by it.

It was Mr Dawes, for instance, who organized the school outings to Krikstone Abbey and other points of consequence in the countryside, and it was on one of these that Moore had his first sight of the stone heads in Methley Church which came to mean so much to him. The region round Castleford gave him, also, an experience which marked him for the rest of his life, though it was only uncovered a year or two ago when a camera team from the Columbia Broadcasting System went up to Yorkshire in connection with a television programme on Moore and his career. While there, they took some shots of the Adle, a huge rock which Moore remembered going to see, at the age of nine or ten, with his father. Today the Adle is in part overgrown with trees, but in 1908 or thereabouts it was entirely bare; and one of the camera team noticed, and Moore later confirmed, that when photographed from a certain angle the Adle was remarkably like the leg-end of the *Two-piece Reclining Figure, no. 1,* which Moore produced more than half a century after his first visit.

By the time Moore was ten or eleven he found that he was getting a great deal of pleasure from drawing classes, and from carving old bits of wood and stone, but nothing had happened to form within him the sense of vocation. But then one day in Sunday school his teacher was pointing the moral that one should always listen to others and try to learn from them. As an example of this he described how when Michelangelo was carving his head of a faun, someone passed by and said 'But that's an old faun. Surely an old faun would have lost some of his teeth?' And so Michelangelo took up his chisel and knocked out two of the faun's teeth. 'So there you are,' said the teacher, 'there's the greatest sculptor in the world ready to take advice from a stranger, just because he'd listened carefully and thought it made sense!'

Moore didn't take much to the moral, one way or the other, and as he had never seen a faun the point about the teeth went for nothing with him. What stuck was the phrase 'the greatest sculptor in the world'. Something about it sounded *right,* in the way that a phrase quite casually spoken, in a context of indifference, can sometimes carry a hidden message that changes a whole life. Thenceforward, if anyone asked what he wanted to be in life, Moore would say 'A sculptor.'

Now, it might seem that he was badly placed to further this ambition. Sculpture as a fine art

could not be studied at first hand any nearer than London, and in Edwardian times there was really nothing in the way of accessible books on the subject, even if at the age of ten or eleven he had known how to get at them. There had never been an artist in the family. The prospects for a full-time sculptor were bleak in any event, and as far as the practicalities of a career were concerned he might as well have said 'I want to be a toreador' for all the hope he had of getting informed direction.

But this is not to say that in the long run, and as seen from today, the auguries were unfavourable. On the contrary: the auspices for Moore the sculptor were almost as good, for anyone who knows how to read them, as they were for Braque, who was born with a paint-brush more or less in his hand, or for Matisse when at the end of his career he turned to the strips of cut-out paper which just happened to be the medium towards which his sixty years of experience had been tending.

Part of the Moore legend insists that he was born into a world which knew nothing of

4

sculpture. This is untrue as a matter of observable fact, and it is untrue to Moore's own experience as he himself has recorded it. There is hardly a country church in England that did not acquire, between the Reformation and the deaths of Chantrey (1841) and Westmacott (1856) something of interest in the way of sculpture. 'Educated' people did not look at these things until a generation ago: but today anyone can make the connection between column and capital, or between the reclining Crusader, and the relevant pieces in Moore's *œuvre*. Of all the strains which go to make up that *œuvre*, this has been least subject to analysis; but Moore himself authorized us to go ahead when he wrote in 1941 of the eleventh-century carvings which he had seen, as a boy, on Yorkshire churches. *As a boy*: those are the words which count most. Moore has always refused to grope around among his earliest memories, and when a German scholar studied his work on psycho-analytical lines he refused even to read the book which resulted, for fear that it dragged into the open sources

best left to work themselves out undisturbed; but there is no doubt that the observation of sculpture formed a part of his life as a boy, and that it was sculpture of a kind altogether grander, and less enfeebled by aestheticizing, than he would have met with at that date in a household where art was much talked of.

At that time it was quite possible to go to art school at the age of fourteen. But when Moore eventually got to Leeds School of Art in September 1919 as an accredited ex-service student, he could only congratulate himself on having missed the years of pointless drudgery which then did duty for art education. The vital thing for a would-be sculptor in Edwardian England was to stay clear of the academic ideal in sculpture and keep alive the instinct of play and the power of unselfconscious invention. This Moore did, as a schoolboy, in circumstances best described in his own words:

Near where we lived in Castleford there was a quarry, and we used to play about with the clay and make what we called touchstone ovens, little square boxes with chimneys and a hole at the side, and we'd fill these with rotten wood and light it and blow on the fire to warm our hands in the winter. And sometimes we'd decorate them with drawings. All our games had a seasonal rotation – whip-and-top time lasted three weeks, for instance – and one of the games that came round was called 'Piggie'. For this, you took a round piece of wood and shaped the ends of it till you could hit it with a stick and make it jump into the air. I very much enjoyed carving the piggie, and of course I was carving and modelling the clay all the time too.

From 'Piggie', the players later turned to a more highly developed game called 'Knurr and Spell'. This also involved wood-carving, in that the ball was first caught in, and later thrown from, an oblong container which ended in a tapering, oblique-angled hand-piece. Recently, when prompted by a biographer to look into the question of these games, Moore made what would in psycho-analytical terms be called a significant connection. He realized, that is to say, that in his middle thirties, when his work was apparently at its most hermetic, the image of 'Knurr and Spell' rose up from his unconscious and took a hand in the Cumberland alabaster *Bird and Egg* (pl. 2) which was one of the most mysterious of his inventions for the year 1934. Here, in fact, were the ball, and the tapering handle, and the oblique angle, and the egg-shaped hollow with the circular hole at the bottom of it in which the ball was to rest. There could hardly be a neater or a more exact illustration of the workings of the unconcious in art.

I doubt, for that matter, if anyone could invent, for that time and that place, a more auspicious beginning for a sculptor than this constant, spontaneous, and enjoyable contact both with the materials of his art and with its social function. Instead of the debased rituals of art school, Moore was occupied with something that fulfilled an immediate social need, however modest: looking for instance at a piece like the *Sculpture to hold* in yew-wood of 1936, it seems to me that this work, though related to Giacometti's, must also have its source in the 'piggies' of Moore's boyhood. Equally, the mysterious block-like carvings of 1936 may relate in part to the early reliefs of Ben Nicholson, who was a close neighbour of Moore's at that time; but

they are also, I think, a sublime variant of the touchstone ovens – square-cut, monolithic, incised and drawn-upon, and instinct with a magic in which 'fine art' has no part.

Moore's family greeted his decision to become a sculptor without even a mandatory minimum of discouragement. His father said no more than that it would be a good thing if he qualified as a teacher, in order to have something to fall back on, and Moore's mother made no comment at all, except to say later, when she saw what gruelling physical work was involved, that she thought he 'might really have found an easier profession'. Moore became a student-teacher in 1915, and in the following year he returned as a teacher to the elementary school which he had attended as a small boy. (Now that there were several teachers in the family, the Moores had moved from 36 Roundhill Road, the house in which he was born, to a larger house in a rather grander neighbourhood: the corner house, that is to say, in Smawthorne Lane.)

It seems, from this distance, as if nothing could break the ordered and smiling round of Castleford life. Moore himself goes so far as to say, in fact, that even the Army, which he joined in 1917, was 'just like a bigger family', in that at first he was the youngest member of his regiment, the Fifteenth London Regiment (Civil Service Rifles). Readers of *Her Privates We* and *Good-bye to All That* would find it difficult to recognize the war of 1914–18 as it appears in Moore's characteristically understated recollections.

For me, the war passed in a romantic haze of hoping to be a hero. Sometimes in France there were three or four days of great danger when you thought there wasn't a chance of getting through, and then all one felt was sadness at having taken so much trouble to no purpose; but on the whole I enjoyed the Army. . . . After I was gassed at Cambrai I was in hospital for three months and it still affects my voice at times, but as they made me a PT instructor afterwards I suppose I must have got pretty fit again.

These are not the words of one marked for life by experiences too dreadful to be set down. What they imply is not insensibility, but rather the armoured equilibrium of one who has already learnt to manage life, even in its more

5 Torso *Plaster for bronze 30 in. 1925 Destroyed*

extravagant manifestations, and how to keep one distant aim consistently in mind.

In point of time, Moore's war service caused a minimum of delay, in that he was demobilized in February 1919, went back to teaching (at the same school) a month later, and in September 1919 was able at last to get to Leeds School of Art on an ex-serviceman's grant. He was just twenty-one years old, therefore, when he reached that crucial phase at which a potential artist's ideas and inclinations and unformed devices come up against the System. That System may be draconic or permissive, deadening or inspired, rigid or improvisatory, but in any event it represents the formed as against the unformed world. Much depends on the student's ability to cope with it and make the most of it.

Moore is categorical in this respect. 'I was very lucky not to have gone to art school until I knew better than to believe what the teachers said.' Forty and fifty years ago there was nothing more dismal than the routines of a provincial art school. Hostility to living art was as intense in Leeds as it was anywhere in England – that is, very intense indeed – and there had lately been trouble about the War Memorial which had been commissioned from Eric Gill for the University, and trouble again about a projected series of decorations which were to have been commissioned for the Victoria Hall. In both these episodes the weight of the attacks bore heaviest upon the Vice-Chancellor of the University, Sir Michael Sadler. Sadler was a collector of quite exceptional discernment: he had bought Cézanne, Gauguin, Daumier, Courbet, and others before 1914, and already in 1912 he had visited Kandinsky in Bavaria and bought a number of his works. Later he turned also to the work of British artists, and from Wilson Steer onwards there were few artists of promise whom he did not go out of his way to help. (For John Piper, in 1925, he was 'the man on earth I most wanted to meet'.) From 1912 to 1924, Sadler gave himself unstintingly to Leeds, and it was Roger Fry who best summed up his achievement when he wrote:

Every time I came to Leeds I got more and more impressed with the work Sir Michael was doing. He had civilized a whole population. The entire spirit had changed from a rather sullen suspicion of ideas to a genuine enthusiastic intellectual and spiritual life. He showed what *can* be done – but very rarely is – by education.

Moore was old enough to pick and choose among what was on offer, and the thing that he chose at once, and held fast to, was the example of Sadler, and of Roger Fry and Clive Bell, and of the one or two other people who went adventuring without prejudice among art of all sorts and all periods. These adventures were still limited and imperfect, by comparison with those now available to the student of art, but they made up for their imperfection by an intensity of excitement not easily recaptured when all experience is to be had for the asking. Moore's consciousness was still in a phase of unbounded expansion in which every new experience was marked 'plus' and the problems of choice and co-ordination had yet to arise. The important thing was still (as Moore wrote in 1935) to get rid of the 'complete domination of later, decadent Greek art as the only standard of excellence'.

This state of affairs continued when Moore won a Royal Exhibition Scholarship in sculpture and went in September 1921 to the Royal College of Art in London. Even today, after nearly fifty years, something of the exhilaration of those first months in London comes across without effort in Moore's conversation.

I was in a dream of excitement. When I rode on the open top of a bus I felt that I was travelling in Heaven almost, and that the bus was floating in the air. And it was Heaven all over again in the evening, in the little room that I had in Sydney Street. It was a dreadful room, the most horrible little room you could imagine, and the landlady gave me the most awful finnan haddock for breakfast every morning, but at night I had my books, and the coffee stall on the Embankment if I wanted to go out to eat, and I knew that not far away I had the National Gallery and the British Museum and the Victoria & Albert with the reference library where I could get at any book I wanted. I could learn about all the sculptures that had ever been made in the world. With the £90 a year that I had in scholarships I was one of the real rich students at the College and I had no worries or problems at all except purely and simply my own development as a sculptor. As to that, there were a whole lot of things that I found out for myself very simply and easily. Once you'd read Roger Fry, the whole thing was there. I went to the British Museum on Wednesday

8 Standing Woman *Walnut 12 in.* 1923 *City Art Gallery, Manchester*

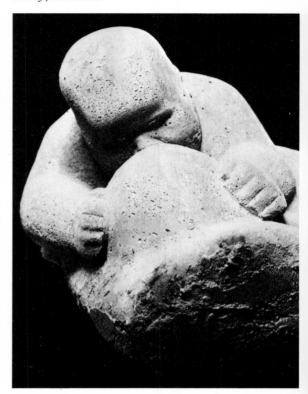

and Sunday afternoons and saw what I wanted to see. It was all quite straightforward.

The R.C.A. at that time had just acquired Sir William Rothenstein as its Principal. What had been primarily a teachers' training college took on quite another character under Rothenstein's directorate. There was, to begin with, a new emphasis on creativity among the students. Rothenstein discouraged the idea that art could be taught by people who had no first-hand experience of what it meant to try, at any rate, to produce a work of art. He was, secondly, a man who looked outwards and into the great world. He was not at all provincial, had known Degas and Rodin and many another great European figure, and kept up a large acquaintance among the *Prominenten* of his own day. He made a point of inviting one or two students up to his house on Sunday evenings: Walter de la Mare was one of many people whom Moore met in this way, and once in 1924, when still a student, Moore found himself standing on the hearth-rug with Ramsay Macdonald, who was then Prime Minister of England.

Rothenstein gave one the sense that there need be no barrier and no limit to what one can embark upon, and that is very important to a young student. Here was I, a student straight from Yorkshire, and it seemed perfectly natural for me to be standing in front of the fire and talking to the Prime Minister.

In this way Rothenstein carried on with a process and an idea which had begun, for Moore, at elementary school: the notion, in short, that a man was what he made himself.

One certain thing about art school is that students learn as much from contact with other students as they do from their teachers. Moore had very few fellow students in the sculpture school – at one time he had a studio and a model for his exclusive use for a whole year – and most of his friends were in the painting school. In his first year he went to Paris with one of them, Raymond Coxon. They had had the idea that instead of reading and re-reading about Cézanne in Roger Fry it would be a good plan to go and see some originals. Rothenstein agreed that they could take off a whole week at Whitsuntide, and he also gave them two or three introductions. One of these

10 Ancient Mexican God Chacmool, the Rain Spirit
Limestone Mexico City

was to Maillol. But when Moore got to Maillol's door he said to himself 'Oh well – he'll be working and he won't want to see me', and he turned and went away. But he did take up the introduction to the Pellerin family, and in this way he and Coxon saw the enormous *Grandes Baigneuses* of Cézanne which is now in the Art Gallery in Philadelphia. 'You know, the ones with the nudes in perspective, lying on the ground, that look as if they were cut out of mountain rock. Seeing that picture, for me, was like seeing Chartres Cathedral. It was one of the big impacts.'

This visit took place in the summer of 1922. Before long Moore began to be conscious for the first time of the tension in his activity which, once resolved, was to be his greatest single strength as an artist. This tension arose from the contrast – some would have said, the contradiction – in style and impetus between the work he was doing at the College and the work he was doing in his spare time in digs. He had gone to the College with what he now calls a 'silly and romantic idea' that art schools and

their teaching were no good, anyway, and that the only sensible thing was to put in an appearance at the College and pursue his serious studies outside. After a month or two he realized that sculptors like Michelangelo and Rodin could draw as well as any of the great painters. He also realized that for practical reasons the only place in which he could learn to draw and model from life was an art school. In this way Moore began to lead what was, in effect, a double life: working from the model in the day-time, and struggling in the evening and at week-ends to develop his powers in an altogether different way.

The routine of the College had its afflictions. There was for instance the 'monthly comp.', in which the students' work was pinned up on the wall and was criticized freely and in public by a senior member of the staff. 'That young man has been feeding on garbage' was the verdict on an early drawing of Moore's which showed the influence of something – Negro or Etruscan art – which was not in the standard College curriculum. ('I'm sorry about that', said

11 Mother and Child *Portland stone 11 in.* 1922 *Private Collection*

Rothenstein to Moore afterwards, 'but it's bound to happen sometimes.') But none of this affected the central fact that he was learning, as he says,

to see form completely: and that's what a sculptor needs. You can draw a tree, or a bit of architecture, or a bit of landscape, or even an animal, and people don't notice – don't feel it, anyway – if you haven't got it quite right. But if you're drawing a human being it's quite different. Critical standards, your own and everyone else's, are infinitely keener. Even if you want to be an abstract sculptor, it's still invaluable to have had that training in drawing the figure. And it's not only training in the literal sense – one can't understand it without being emotionally involved. It is a deep, strong, fundamental struggle to understand oneself as much as to understand what one's drawing.

However much a European artist may talk, as Moore did later, about 'getting the Greek spectacles off one's nose', there is no doubt that the struggle which he was describing is a European struggle, and one which lies somewhere in the unconscious of everyone who has been brought up as a European and given even so much as wry, resentful attention to the established hierarchy of Western art. The balance of the erect human body, which Moore evokes as eloquently in conversation as in his life drawings of the 1920s, is reflected in the balance of the marks a Leonardo or a Michelangelo makes on the paper. There is, that is to say, a central tradition, and it can't but pull strongly at any student who gives all of himself to the task of drawing.

In the 1960s every sculpture-student has a built-in awareness of all the other elements which have contributed to the emancipation of sculpture. In the 1920s the situation was entirely different. Very few people had a clear grasp of what had been done by Brancusi, for instance, and although many young artists had a confused and partial idea of the sources of energy inherent in what was then called 'primitive' art it was quite another matter to incorporate these energies into work that made sense. There is no such thing as the painless incorporation within a work of art of elements taken whole from an alien culture. Yet the 1920s were the heyday of the mixed marriage of idiom, and thought, and intention in every

department of the arts. What is *The Waste Land*, if not a multiple mixed marriage of this sort? By naming the greatest poem of the twentieth century I have, however, given a misleading impression of the degree of success to which such mixed marriages normally attained. Time has dealt severely with nearly all the 'experimental' work of the period. It would be embarrassing to list the casualties incurred in poetry, in the novel, in drama, in music, and in the fine arts by ventures which relied on the outward aspects of experiment, without corresponding to any profound emotional thrust and without having striven to assimilate and acclimatize modes of expression conceived elsewhere and, as often as not, at a great distance in time. But the year of Moore's first visit to Paris was, in spite of all this, the year in which *Ulysses* and *The Waste Land* were first published; Picasso had painted the *Three Musicians* the year before, Braque was perfecting his 'Chimneypiece' series, Brancusi had just finished his *Torso of a Young Man*, and Klee and Kandinsky were at the Weimar

Bauhaus. There was enough of superlative merit in the output of the year to put any young man on his mettle. But equally evident was the ever-widening gap between the work of living art which came off and the work of living art which didn't. There was a topmost level of achievement, as there had always been: below that level there was only chaos and confusion. The minor master or acceptable epigone, so common in earlier epochs, had been swept off the board altogether since the beginnings of analytical cubism. Till 1908 or thereabouts it was possible to make out a modest case for Trouillebert as against Corot, for Lebourg as against Monet, for Willy Finch even, as against Seurat: what they did was decent enough, provided that the claim was not set too high. But for Gleizes as against Picasso and Braque no case can be made, because the misunderstanding of the principles involved in the work of the major artists is total and irreparable. Nietzsche's remark that 'every great human being is a finale' is relevant, once again, to the major figures of the time. Attempts at resuscitation have proved again and again that there just is not, any longer, a level of acceptable minor achievement, some way below but within hailing distance of the giants. These giants have kicked down the ladder, once and for all, and it has to be set up somewhere else.

But if it is easy to tidy up, from a safe distance, the historical situation of the early 1920s, it was quite a different thing to live through it. The living artist is not primarily a historian, though he may have insights that a historian must envy, and it is not by thinking about history that he will win a place in it. Franz Kline put this point very well, not long before he died: 'You don't paint the way someone, observing your life, thinks you *have* to paint. You paint the way you have to in order to give. Someone will look at it and say it is the product of knowing, but it has nothing to do with knowing. It has to do with giving.' How to give, and what to give, were the fundamental problems for Moore in his twenties.

Like every other young artist, gifted or not, he began by trying on other people's hats and seeing how well they fitted him.

When I first came to London I was aware of Brancusi, Gaudier-Brzeska, Modigliani and the early Epstein, and of all that that direction in sculpture stood for. I couldn't help – nobody can after all – being a part of my own time. But then I began to find my own direction, and one thing that helped, I think, was the fact that Mexican sculpture had more excitement for me than negro sculpture. As most of the other sculptors had been more moved by negro sculpture this gave me a feeling that I was striking out on my own.

Among the European artists whom Moore names, Gaudier-Brzeska seems to me to have had an influence which is clear in the early carvings of animals (pls. 3, 4) and clearer still in the tender little *Torso* of 1925–6 (pl. 5) and the *Suckling Child* in cast concrete of 1927 (pl. 7) both of which can be related to known pieces by Gaudier (pl. 6). Epstein can be detected in the flattened, frieze-like planes of more than one early composition (pl. 4), and when Moore was invited in 1926 to make some decorative compositions to go with a fountain the result had a certain kinship with Epstein. One or two very early pieces reveal that Moore had looked carefully at African sculpture – doubtless as a result of reading in Roger Fry that 'certain nameless savages' had produced 'great sculpture – greater, I think, than anything England produced even in the Middle Ages'. But Africa left no lasting mark. Egypt stood for something, also, in the imposing *Seated Figure* (pl. 9) of 1924.

With Mexico, the case was quite different. And although Moore's remarks in 1941 on Mexican art have often been quoted I think that they must be set down again here.

Mexican sculpture, as soon as I found it seemed to me true and right, perhaps because I at once hit on similarities in it with some eleventh-century carvings I had seen as a boy on Yorkshire churches. Its 'stoniness', by which I mean its truth to material, its tremendous power without loss of sensitiveness, its astonishing variety and fertility of form-invention, and its approach to a full three-dimensional conception of form, make it unsurpassed in my opinion by any other period of stone sculpture.

Given so strong a scent, even the most languid hound could hardly fail to see something of the chase. Moore's closest Mexican affinity, in most people's view, is with the reclining statue *Chacmool, the Rain Spirit* (pl. 10). This is in

13 Anthropomorphic Statue from Guatemala *height 44 in.* 300 BC *Musée de l'Homme, Paris*

limestone, and life-size; it comes from Chicèn Itzà, and is now in Mexico City. The Chacmool statue can, in effect, be seen as the source of many of Moore's reclining figures, and as the source of what he has called his obsession with the subject in general. But an even closer, though short-lived affinity might be traced between the Portland stone *Mother and Child* (pl. 11), which dates from the summer of 1922 and is Moore's earliest surviving independent carving, and the British Museum's figure (pl. 12) of Xochipilli, the *Flower Prince of the Aztecs*. The Moore has a kind of edgy, irritable quality which I suspect has as much to do with the artist's state of mind, and with the still limited development of his gifts, as with any expressive intention. One has only to compare the relaxed eloquence of the pose in the Mexican figure, and the rich and confident handling of its lower legs, to see that Moore was still very much a student.

But, over and above the rude power which the Moore already gives off, there is a blockishness which was to characterize several important early carvings by Moore. He seems to have wanted to disturb the original character of the block as little as possible – partly, no doubt, in order to preserve its monumental quality, and partly from the feeling, now largely obsolete, that 'truth to the material' was one of the most important things about a sculpture. The forms seem almost to hug the block, as if to defend it against the sculptor's attack: there is, in fact, an almost palpable struggle between that sacred object, the block, and the image which the sculptor wishes to impose upon it. Today all this seems archaic: the idea of choosing a beautiful or an intrinsically rewarding material has been turned inside-out and the artist often aims either to deny, or to metamorphose, the nature of his materials, or to regenerate substances for which the world has no dignified name. But in the first quarter of this century a real moral superiority was ascribed to direct carving. (Carving was so rare in art schools that the examinations passed by Moore during his years in the sculpture school in Leeds were specifically in 'modelling', it being taken for granted that this was the subject which would be presented.) Epstein and Eric Gill were both, in their different ways, champions of the idea that bronze-casting was an erratic and slightly discreditable short-cut to achievement, and that only the stone, marble, or wood which had been carved from start to finish by the sculptor's own hand could be ranked as true sculpture. One or two European artists – Brancusi, Modigliani, Zadkine, Barlach – could be adduced in support of this, though it must sometimes have occurred to people that Rodin had hardly ever had a chisel in his hand. In England the point of view had overtones of our native Arts and Crafts movement; inherent in it, quite clearly, was the idea of 'truth to material'. Moore has since modified his opinions, realizing that the artist must set truth to himself higher than truth to his material, and that too great a love and respect for the material may inhibit and even stultify a sculptor at some vital stage in his work. But up till 1939 virtually all Moore's three-dimensional work was carved. Of the first 200 items in the Sylvester catalogue, fewer than 20 have been cast in bronze: and of these several have only been cast since 1945. The act of carving has, in itself, a dramatic, all-risking irrevocable quality, and this gives it a dignity not quite to be rivalled by the act of modelling, where it is always possible to have, and to act upon, second thoughts. 'Truth to material', in those distant days, was the beginning of integrity in sculpture.

Moore had from the start, then, a certain attitude to his material. Each new piece, between 1922 and 1939, was to be an encounter with a particular substance: marble, Portland stone, Mansfield stone, Pynkado wood, Cumberland alabaster, ironstone, African wonderstone, Corsehill stone, Travertine marble, Ancaster stone, ebony, beechwood, Ham Hill stone, Hornton stone, Hoptonwood stone, verde di prato, walnut wood, serpentine, Bath stone, painted slate. Nothing in these encounters was taken for granted.

He also had a certain attitude to his sources. What mattered was not so much 'the Mexican inspiration', for instance, as Moore's awareness of what he later called 'the common world-language of forms'. What he needed was not so much the stimulus of alien imagery as the enfranchisement which comes from knowing that one's own earliest memories are part of the unity of all human experience. Any lively young person can run through the panorama of recorded art and pick out the things which excite him: but what results, on that level, is a jumpy, un-ballasted art. What marks the serious artist for a lifetime is the authorization which comes from the knowledge that an illimitable repertory of images is within each of us, only asking to be brought upwards to consciousness.

Finally, Moore had, even as a student, the beginnings of a style. Whether the weight of the style would balance the weight of the self must have been continually in doubt. He had the material, he had the sources, and he had the beginnings of a style. But what to do with it all? What myths, legends, attitudes, and exorcisms to conjure forth? What to say, and how to say it? What, in a word – in Kline's word – what to *give*? That was still a problem, and it was hardly nearer to resolution in the experimental carvings of his student days than it was in the variant of a relief by Domenico Rosselli which he made in 1922. Before he could give himself entirely, and before he could even know what he wanted to give, the two sides of his life as a student must be drawn nearer together and the sedulous workman in the life-class be mated, somehow, with the investigator of 'the common world-language of forms'. This mating took place, slowly and painfully, as a result of the Travelling Scholarship which he was awarded in 1924, and which took him, in the first six months of 1925, to many places in northern and central Italy.

II 1924-1931

The year 1924 was of cardinal importance to Moore. To begin with, it was the year in which he won the Travelling Scholarship which took him to Italy. It was also the year in which he first profited by that invaluable English institution, the part-time teaching job.

Without such a job, he might have been forced back into the provinces, with only intermittent access to the museums, the exhibitions, the libraries and the personal contacts which had brought him on, as they bring every young artist on, since he arrived in London in the autumn of 1921. The job was, moreover, in the Royal College itself. Derwent Wood, the Professor of Sculpture at the R.C.A. had resigned after a disagreement with the Principal, who later referred to him in his memoirs as 'an excellent modeller, the most scholarly of the academic sculptors'. Reading round this encomium, one might infer that Moore, an unacademic carver, cannot greatly have regretted the change. Rothenstein would have liked to appoint Epstein as his successor, but that idea was scotched by the Permanent Under-Secretary at the Board of Education, whose letter on the subject is a classic instance of Establishment attitudes. 'To appoint Epstein',

he wrote, 'would be a very perilous experiment and might cause us considerable embarrassment. For a Professor we would want not only a genius (as to which I am no authority) but also character; and I am not sure that character in a place of this kind is not of greater importance.' As Moore's genius was not yet in question, and his character appeared to be all that could be wished, no objection was raised to his appointment as Assistant in the Sculpture Department.

This stood for security of a kind which then seemed impregnable. Moore was paid £240 a year for a total of 66 days' teaching. He had, therefore, 299 days in which to get on with his own work in conditions of financial equilibrium. He did, in fact, devote himself to his students to the point of dreaming about them, night after night, and fretting continually as to whether he was or was not telling them the right things; and after ten years he was thoroughly tired of teaching. But meanwhile, and at a time when the people in England who owned a piece of modern sculpture could be numbered on one hand, there were still five days of every week, and nineteen complete weeks of every year, in which he had no

15 A. DERAIN Homme Accroupi *Stone 12 in.* 1907
Galerie Leiris, Paris

obligation to anything except his own sculpture. To that extent the teaching job was an immediate and unmixed gain.

The Italian journey, which began in January 1925, was quite another matter. Moore had not in the first instance wanted to go to Italy at all. But the Travelling Scholarship was awarded 'for the study of the Old Masters', and not for the furtherance of the winner's own work, and it had always been taken for granted that the Italian Old Masters were the only Old Masters and that Italy was the only place to study them. If Moore's application to spend the time in Paris, or alternatively in Germany, was turned down it was partly for this reason and partly because there was no accepted means of paying the money in any country but Italy. 'Either I went to Italy', Moore said later, 'or I didn't get the scholarship. So I went to Italy.'

He left behind him a piece half completed: the Hornton stone *Mother and Child* (pl. 14) which is now in Manchester. This redoubtable piece is the first to signal, on any substantial scale (it is 22½ inches high), his preoccupation

with forms of female beauty that are full, heavy, solid, and slow. He once said himself that 'There are specific kinds of sensibility, belonging to distinct psychological types': and he has followed this principle to the extent of not attempting subjects which lie outside his own kind of sensibility. The Manchester *Mother and Child* forecasts, already, that inimitable broody quality which finds its most majestic expression in the UNESCO carving (pls. 175, 176). But to Moore himself the Manchester piece now exemplifies the shortcomings of the doctrine of 'truth to material'. Essentially, he feels, it is still a block of stone with the corners sliced off, and the nature of that block is not so much set free as mutilated by the sculptor's activity. The forms now strike Moore as having been buried one within the other, the head and arm of the baby as having been stuck on, and the structure as a whole as being external, not internal. The necks are still packed away inside the stone. The faceting of the forms derives from Cubism, but the forms themselves hug the block. It is, in fact, as if the piece had turned out to symbolize the block's resistance to the artist. (Derain, working in stone as early as 1907, had met with the same difficulty.)

The Manchester *Mother and Child* would have been a difficult piece, in any circumstances, for a young artist in the early 1920s. Sculptures of that date by other and older 'advanced' artists – Frank Dobson, for instance – were usually made up of sharp-angled, jagged, abrupt planes that cut back and forth. Moore's piece, on the contrary, is marked *maestoso*. It is midway – that much we can see now – between the aggressive and obviously 'experimental' pieces of 1923 and the suave utterance which he had mastered in the carving (done long before he saw Italy) after Domenico Rosselli. Eventually the tension between the two was happily resolved, but at the time it was torturous.

The first effect of Moore's Italian tour was to make it impossible for him to work at all. He could neither go on as before, nor start on a new tack that had any coherence. At a time when Moore's 'modernity' was his most obvious and controversial characteristic it was difficult to point to any palpable effect of the trip on his output. Today it seems to us one of the vital dates in his career.

Initially, in January 1924, he tried to act

16 FRANK DOBSON Seated Torso 1923 *Musée de l'Homme, Paris*

according to the view that the Renaissance, like the fifth century B.C. in Greece, had been overplayed. But this could not work as a general proposition: no fair-minded and inquisitive person could live in Italy for four months and confine himself to the traces of Byzantium. His scholarship was intended, too, to provide a miscellaneous grounding in Italian art. Moore did what he now calls 'four months of taking off one's hat, as one had to, to Michelangelo and Donatello and Masaccio, and then going on to Venice and seeing Titian and Tintoretto and the others'. This did lasting damage to the idea that what mattered most was non-European art. Not that the idea was ever dropped, or has been dropped now: Moore knows the British Museum and the Musée de l'Homme in Paris as few people know them. But the two enthusiasms had somehow to be reconciled.

Simultaneously, the fact of being away from England for the first time caused him to think over what he missed, or didn't miss, and to formulate his ambitions for the future. He wrote back to Sir William Rothenstein that he aimed to be an artist in England and not outside it, 'working and carving in the big tradition of sculpture'. (Donatello the modeller seemed to him 'the beginning of the end'.)

I am beginning to get England into perspective – I think I shall return a violent patriot. If this scholarship does nothing else for me, it will have made me realize what treasures we have in England, and how inspiring is our English landscape. I do not wonder that the Italians have no landscape school – I have a great desire, almost an ache, for the sight of a tree that can be called a tree – for a tree with a trunk. [This feeling for home was a part of the general commotion of Moore's Italian journey.] I see now [he said later] that it's dangerous for young people to stop doing their own work and concentrate for a long period on other people's. In Italy there was just too much richness, too much to sort out all at once. I knew, even then, that it had to be done, and that the richer an artist's work was, the more he would turn out to have garnered from all over. If you take Cézanne, for instance, you remember how much he owned to Tintoretto and El Greco and Daumier and Pissarro. And I believe that the bigger a person is, the more he will use his

17 The goddess Xochiquetzal, Mexican *30 in.* 15th century *Musée de l'Homme, Paris*

experience of other people's work when he comes to do his own. But at that time, in 1924, it was an ordeal.

It was an ordeal that began in Paris, with Moore's first sight of a Mexican reclining figure; and it went on, week after week, with the steady and painful reconstitution of one idea after another. Every morning for a month Moore would go to the Brancacci Chapel in Florence to get a hold on Masaccio before setting off to see anything else; and as he went on from one great Italian centre to another he faced something that grew steadily more baffling: the problem of how to get the two great sculptural achievements, European and non-European, to co-exist. His Italian experience was by no means comprehensive – several of the most powerful impacts, like that of the Rondanini *Pietà* and of the Giovanni Pisanos in Pisa, were to come in later years – but it was enough to bring him to an unexpected, complete, and agonizing halt.

When his own work did get going again it resulted, naturally enough, in pieces which have an uneasy and a transitional look. In the *Two Heads* (pl. 18) of 1924–5 the wind blows in strongly from the Cyclades. The chunky *Maternity* of 1924 (pl. 19) has to do with the problem of the block. Other pieces relate to what was then called the 'modernistic' European idiom of the day. Two long-destroyed figures, the *Torso* of 1925 and a *Reclining Figure* of 1926, showed the tender side of Moore's nature for once uppermost: significantly, both were modelled and not carved. They also announced the two major themes of Moore's maturity, the vertical and the recumbent figure, in naturalistic and purely European terms. (Gaudier for the one, Maillol for the other, could have stood as godfathers.) What it is difficult to find, anywhere in these works, is the authentic Moore-note.

But by 1926, and beyond a doubt by 1927, it begins to ring out: not interruptedly, but in one or two pieces of primordial importance. The little *Torso* in African wood, for instance (pl. 20), is the ancestor of all Moore's upright figures. During the autumn and winter of 1927, again, Moore was working on the verde di prato *Head and Shoulders* (pl. 21) which is to my mind the first outright masterpiece of his career. For the first time, he achieved fully

three-dimensional forms which are consistently memorable: the piece is impossible to photograph, in that a photograph can isolate only one of its aspects. The organization of the forms is at once subtler, more delicate, and more radical than anything Moore had attempted before. But those forms were still, essentially, Cubist facets embedded in one another. It was as if Moore had made a drawing of the subject in Cubist idiom, wrapped it round the block, and given an almighty squeeze. Beautiful as the result was (and the handling of nose, eye, mouth, brow, shoulder, and breast is one of the most tender of Moore's inspirations), it still lacked something of the realization-from-inwards at which he was aiming. (The piece is, by the way, infinitely more expressive, in human terms, than all but a very few of the paintings done in France, or anywhere else, in late cubist idiom). The forms were coaxed, not commanded: it may be significant, in this context, that Moore has a lifelong admiration for Seurat, who seems to him to have been the only artist since the Renaissance to have evolved a new and valid kind of drawing. Seurat perfected a way, when drawing, of cherishing the form continuously, coaxing it forward from darkness into light, never losing it for an instant as he lets the light reveal its fullness and roundness: in all this, there is something of the sculptural ideal.

Both the African wood *Torso* and the verde di prato *Head and Shoulders* were quintessentially human in their idiom: that is to say, everything in them can be traced to specific elements in the human body, and their areas of maximum tenderness correspond, equally, to our normal experience of that body. No violence is done, in either piece, and the body is not used metaphorically. This went on being true, right up to 1939, of quite a number of Moore's gentler and more obviously tender pieces. It was true of the single heads, and of the masks, and of the images of maternity, and of some of the most elegant of his standing and seated figures. But it is not with these that he broke through to the forefront of modern sculpture: for that, less comfortable pieces were needed.

Eventually the conflict between the European and non-European idioms was resolved. Moore went on, right through the 1930s, with pieces that owed allegiance to one side or the other,

18 Two Heads *Mansfield stone 13½ in. 1924–5 Miss Mary Moore*

but it was in the long series of Reclining Figures that he first managed to reconcile the two. There, too, he developed an idea which helped to make him famous: the notion of the human body as a metaphor for landscape. (Many years later, as will be seen, he reversed this concept and began to work on landscape as a metaphor for the human body.) I suspect, though I have no grounds for asserting it, that one of the initial germs for the landscape idea was a passage in Roger Fry's early 'Essay in Aesthetics'. Talking of Michelangelo's *Tondo* in the Uffizi, Fry says:

When we find a group of figures so arranged that the planes have a sequence comparable in breadth and dignity to the mouldings of the earth mounting by clearly-felt gradations to an overtopping summit, innumerable instinctive reactions are brought into play.

'Innumerable instinctive reactions': the secret of Moore's command over a large public lies in his ability to release these reactions. And he does this by calling upon (to quote him verbatim) 'those universal shapes to which everybody is subconsciously conditioned and to which they can respond if their conscious control does not shut them off'. A phrase of Gaudier's about mountains being 'sculptural energy' had always seemed to Moore to be worth many an hour of drawing from casts, and by the spring of 1929 he was able to do something about it. From March until May of that year he was at work on the brown Hornton stone *Reclining Figure* (pl. 25) which is now in Leeds. It was not his biggest work to date: he had just finished an eight-foot-long decorative figure, more relief than sculpture, for the Underground building by St James's Park Station; but it was his most ambitious attempt at a three-dimensional figure on what is – and this is too often forgotten – one of the standard themes of European art.

How, for instance, are we to look at the Leeds *Reclining Figure*? In some ways it marks a regression towards direct Mexican influence. In the tremendous heaviness of the right leg and foot, in the stiff and unarticulated right angles of the right shoulder and arm, in the failure of the figure to detach itself from the block, this is a backward-looking piece: in these respects the block has still the upper hand of the artist. But

whereas the Mexican figure of Chacmool is basically a silhouette, and could from a plastic point of view be almost as imposing in low relief, the Leeds figure is designed quite differently, with the left arm standing free from the block and a cavernous opening between the knees to announce one of the artist's now most familiar themes. It is a piece which looks forward a very long way. If we jump ahead, for instance, as far as the post-war *Reclining Figure* in the same material we shall find that although in 1946–7 Moore brought the whole of the left side of the body clear of the ground, turned the right arm and the right leg into a single and continuous form, and in general avoided all naturalistic emphasis, he kept, in essentials, the pose and the general feeling of 1929.

With the Leeds piece, and those which followed it on the same theme, Moore attached himself to a great European tradition. That tradition is exemplified by the Bernini fountain in the Piazza Navona in Rome, the Donner fountain of river-goddesses in the Mehlmarkt in Vienna, Coysevox's Dordogne at Versailles,

20 Torso *African wood carving 19¼ in.* 1927 *Marlborough Fine Art, New York*

21 Head and Shoulders *Verde di prato 18 in.* 1928 *Dr H. Roland*

22 CANOVA Pauline Borghese as Venus *White marble 6 ft. 6 in.* 1805–8 *Galleria Borghese, Rome*

23 RAFAEL DONNER The River Ybbs *Barockmuseum, Vienna*

Canova's *Pauline Borghese as Venus*, Ingres's *Grande Odalisque* and, more recently, Picasso's *Le Printemps*. Prop the human body up on one elbow and you simply can't fail to get a composition that rises and falls in a continuously exciting line: that is the lesson of these works, for all the diversity of intent and occasion and style which distinguishes them one from the other. The Picasso, in particular, comes from a moment in his career which was particularly rich in sculptural suggestion: in 1920 and 1921, while preoccupied with the theme of women bathers, he struck off image after image which was to turn up again not long afterwards in the work of others. Two paintings, especially, seem to me to relate to transitional work by Moore: the *Deux Baigneuses*, dated 28 April 1920, and *Le Printemps* of 1920. Echoes of *Le Printemps* can, in fact, be found in Moore's work as late as the Dartington *Memorial Figure* of 1945; and, in general, Picasso's preoccupation in the early 1920s with heavy-limbed female nudes is one which exactly fitted Moore's needs at the time.

From time to time throughout his career Moore has had temporary obsessions: periods, that is to say, during which one particular subject was explored over and over again.

One has obsessions of that sort. You don't ever want to repeat an experience that you've had once while making a sculpture, but yet the idea keeps coming back and back at you and you have to do something about it. And if you're keyed up as you ought to be when you're doing sculpture you get into such a state of comprehension, or appreciation, of everything around you that the only way is to concentrate on that one idea. If you don't do that, it is almost impossible to go on living. If you let everything in, and if you try to follow up all the ideas for sculpture that come flooding in at such times, you'd just burst. You know how when Mondrian had a wonderful studio in Paris, overlooking the Seine, he had the windows boarded up so that he wouldn't get ideas that distracted him from what he was doing? Well, I couldn't do that, but I understood why he had to do it.

The period of 1929–39 is rich, as will be seen, in brief obsessions of the kind that had to be worked through and got out of the way. But

24 North Wind. Decoration for London Underground
station *Portland stone length 8 ft.* 1929 *St James's Park
Underground Station, London*

25 Reclining Figure *Brown Hornton stone 33 in.* 1929
City Art Gallery and Museum, Leeds

26 Mask *Cast concrete* $7\frac{3}{4}$ *in.* 1929 *Unknown*

the obsession with the Reclining Figure has stayed with Moore for ever. As I have already indicated, he is not all given to auto-analysis and likes, on the contrary, to allow the unconscious to get on with its work without intrusion. To this end, few things are more helpful than subject-matter which allows of unlimited forays from a given and permanent base.

I want to be quite free [he said] of having to find a 'reason' for doing the Reclining Figures, and freer still of having to find a 'meaning' for them. The vital thing for an artist is to have a subject that allows to try out all kinds of formal ideas – things that he doesn't yet know about for certain but wants to experiment with, as Cézanne did in his 'Bathers' series. In my case the reclining figure provides chances of that sort. The subject-matter is *given*. It's settled for you, and you know it and like it, so that within it, within the subject that you've done a dozen times before, you are free to invent a completely new form-idea.

After completing the Leeds figure in May 1929, Moore embarked upon a period of tremendous fertility, in which carving after carving came from the studio – Sylvester catalogues more than twenty for the year 1930 – and the long blockage occasioned by the Italian journey was cleared away once and for all. Moore clearly felt free to experiment in any way he liked. Something in this may have been due to the enthusiasm of the fellow artists who had supported him, most notably, at his first one-man show in 1928 at Dorothy Warren's gallery. Epstein, Augustus John, and Henry Lamb were among those who bought from this show, and the fact of being presented by the vivid and venturesome Miss Warren (who was responsible, around the same time, for showing D. H. Lawrence's paintings) must also have helped to place Moore as an artist of consequence. Many people, in any case, were glad to buy Moore drawings from Miss Warren at the asking price of £1 net.

During this period of intense stylistic activity Moore seems at first sight to have been jumping all over the place and trying his hand at everything from the cast concrete Masks of 1929 (pl. 26), in which there lingers something of the grand frontal approach of Easter Island, to pieces like the Birley half-length of 1931 in veined alabaster (pl. 27), where an extreme

sweetness and evident 'beauty' represent Moore's love of fine material at its most voluptuous. These were trends never to be repeated, like that of the lead Seated Figure of 1930, since destroyed, which is the only instance of his having made a sculpture in a style directly parallel to that of his drawings from life. In 1929–30 there were curious Profiled Heads and a whole group of Maternities. In one and the same year, 1931, half-length figures naturalistically modelled, with even some attempt at characterization, contrasted with a figure in which the head was a tapered oval with two white circles incised upon it, one inside the other. Looking back at twenty-five years' distance, it is of course easy to see which of these was central, and which was peripheral, to Moore's ambition: at the time they seemed to balance one another. And if in time the naturalistic element dropped out almost entirely, it is also possible to see, from today's point of vantage, that the ironstone *Mother and Child* (a mere five inches in height) is the precursor of the Stringed Basket Figures of 1939, which at the time seemed so hermetic. For what is at stake, in both cases, if not the notion of a single flowing and coherent form, roughly ovoid in shape and resting as lightly as possible upon its base?

One or two portrait drawings by Moore exist, and in one or two sculptures dated *c.* 1929–31 there is, as I have said, something like a shot at characterization. Early reclining figures give the head a degree of naturalistic definition which later dropped away from Moore's intentions, and there is among most of Moore's heads a shared wary alertness, a suggestion of ears cocked and eyes turned in vigilance. But in general it is of Moore, as much as of his great predecessor, that we are reminded when we read in Adrian Stokes's book on Michelangelo that 'faces are of much less significance to him than torsoes' and that 'the human frame, rather than the features, represents the person'. This being so, a naturalistic head like the one on the Ottawa *Reclining Woman* of 1930 (pl. 28) has an effect of noble incongruity: it is as if one of the Masks of the previous year or two had jumped down off the wall and got itself into the sculpture when no one was looking. Similarly, the powerfully-modelled breasts and hands of the Ottawa figure contrast with the single scooped-out form that stands for

31 Figure *Beechwood 9 in. 1931 Tate Gallery, London*   32 Composition *Green Hornton stone 19 in. 1931 Mrs Irina Moore*

33 PICASSO Head *Oil on canvas 28¼ in. × 23½ in.*
1929 *Galerie Beyeler, Basel*

legs and feet, and with the summary incisions that hesitate on the edge of indicating toes.

A reclining figure in Corsehill stone of the same year, now lost and probably destroyed, demonstrated even more clearly the transitional stage at which Moore then was: the breasts stood erect in a manner to which Nature could never aspire, but the right hand had sunk into the form that ran uninterruptedly from the elbow to the top of the breast and manifested itself by five grooved incisions like pencils laid flat in wet sand. A third reclining figure of 1930 (pl. 29) is of especial interest in that it shows Moore experimenting with an arabesque-form that embraces the whole figure, as if drawn almost with a single movement of the pencil. It includes, also, the first of the eloquent holes in his Reclining Figure series: and although it is a hole formed quite naturally by the crooking of the right arm it is a speaking hole, as opposed to an anatomical incident: a hole, that is to say, which rhymes with the other ovals in the composition. This piece is of interest, thirdly, for the fact that Moore was trying to get the figure free of the base: there is an elasticity in the woman's body, and an eloquence which is not at all (as it is in some earlier figures) the eloquence of an unusually dramatic sack of coals.

The lesson of a piece such as this must have been, I think, that it was by granting his sculptures the broadest possible independence that Moore was likely to get what he wanted. In the half-length semi-naturalistic figures of 1930–1, for instance, there are always beautiful passages in which Moore redistributes the relative importance of one part of the anatomy as against another and achieves, by doing so, a new kind of monumentality. But there is usually, also, a region at the bottom of the piece where the body ceases to be carved and just comes to an end, like a clothes-peg stuck into the earth. Moore would have found a way out of this impasse in the end, but meanwhile these were sculptures in which the plastic interest gave out an inch or two before the eye got down to the base; greater satisfaction was to be had where Nature had solved the problem: in full-length figures like the *Seated Girl* of 1931 in anhydrite stone (pl. 30), for instance.

This problem was not resolved in the beech-wood *Figure* (pl. 31) of 1931, but this figure is of great historical interest on more than one

ground. It is, to begin with, one of the last small wooden sculptures in which the eloquence of the graining and the eloquence of the formal idea are one. Next, it introduces, in the terraced form of the breasts, a plastic idea which was to come out to royal effect in the Northampton *Madonna* of 1943–4. Thirdly, in giving a Romanesque arch-form to the diaphragm, Moore looked forward even further to the great Standing Reliefs of the 1950s whose most stirring feature is the enormous commotion, associated in life with a supreme degree of sexual fulfilment, in precisely this region of the body.

Another feature of 1931 – the most fruitful year to date in Moore's career – is the arrival of themes metamorphosed successfully from Picasso. I stress 'successfully' because most English borrowings from this source have a look of absurdity. Like everyone else who wanted to know what was going on in modern art at that time, Moore went to Paris as often as he could. There, and from such French art magazines as reached London, he knew more or less what Picasso was up to. He owned, for example, a copy of the Picasso number of *Documents* (1930) in which the work of the previous few years was well illustrated; and the Hornton stone *Composition* of 1931 (pl. 32) was undoubtedly provoked by Picasso's beach scenes of the late 1920s. But although there can be no doubt of the source of the motif, the interest of the piece for Moore lay rather, as he says, 'in the attempt to get one round form to exist inside another, in stone, and stay alive'. Moore was now a grown artist, and an emancipated one, and the attitude to the block which had satisfied him in the early 1920s did not satisfy him now. In this *Composition* he aimed to get clear of the tyranny of the block and to turn the solid square stone into something that existed in independent reality. Picasso's many bathers have a grotesque, elephantine quality: dancing on the beach, identified with the ball that they toss skywards, they have themselves an inflated, rubbery, balloonish appearance; and this Moore has most ingeniously carried over into the stone by constantly varying the axes of his composition, splaying and tilting his feet and arms and retaining only that constant sign of the period, the crooked and right-angled elbow. Elements from earlier sculptures remain here and there: vestigial toes, breast-forms that stand erect,

34 Reclining Figure *Lead length 17 in.* 1931
Zimmerman Collection

tender rounded back-forms that could be those of mother and high-held child. But this is a piece, and a coherent form, that exists in its own right. For the first time, too, Moore has managed to get the sculpture itself almost free of the base, suggesting by the shadowed hollow at its foot that it had come to rest momentarily, much as a thrown ball pauses for an instant in the sand. This is the piece, as it seems to me, in which Moore for the first time found the vein of meaningful ambiguity which has been the source of all that is finest in his later *œuvre*. The little *Double Head* of 1928 had been a ranging shot for something of this sort, in that it presented an image which carries imaginative conviction, even if nothing in Nature corresponds to it; but Moore was not then quite able to deal arbitrarily with Nature's *données*. The solemn, corporeal quality of his life drawings (pl. 81) was carried over into the sculptures. By 1931 he could do what he liked, provided always that he knew what it was.

The Reclining Figure benefited also from the climate of assurance which comes over Moore's work in 1931. The most curious of the series to date, if not the most homogeneous, is the Zimmerman *Reclining Figure* in lead of that year (pl. 34). As David Sylvester pointed out in his notes to the Tate Gallery exhibition of Henry Moore in 1951, this figure is less audacious, less constantly radical, than at least one drawing of the period; but it is, even so, a notably venturesome piece. Behind the dinosaur-like head the rear arm has the form of an eighteenth-century chair-leg. The chest is opened up and traversed by what could be either a preliminary draft for the stringed figures of the later 1930s or an afterglow of the guitar-form which dominates so much of Cubist painting. The figure has flipper-like lower legs and feet, and its stance is at a far remove from the slumped, inert, monolithic posture of the earlier Reclining Figures. Consistent it is not: but it crackles with confident invention.

35 Mother and Child *Green Hornton stone 35 in.* 1932
Sir Robert Sainsbury

III 1930-1939

Moore in his twenties had to puzzle things out more or less by himself, and to that extent it is reasonable to study him in isolation. But art is in the last resort a social activity, and no great work of art was ever produced in a social vacuum. There is no such thing as a masterpiece that was executed without regard for what other artists were doing and had already done: or even, to a lesser extent, without regard for what other human beings might one day want to see. The repercussions and reverberations may be too slight for our consciousness to take note of them; they may, equally, be prime facts of existence. But just as every human being has to adjust to other human beings, so every work of art has to adjust to other works of art. It can be done at a distance, but most of the great advances in modern art have been made by small groups of relatively young people who knew each other very well. This is true of the Nabis, the Fauves, the Cubists, the German Expressionists, the Dadaists, the Surrealists, the constructivists, the first and second New York schools: and if there are apparent exceptions – if Seurat, Klee, Arp, Duchamp, Brancusi, and Giacometti seem to have been quite alone at vital moments in their evolution – they too

were supremely aware of the general situation of art, and of the points at which they could press their gifts home. And the crucial moment in the development of any artist, great or small, is the moment at which the private world of the studio must be adjusted to the world outside.

Another general point that should be made at this stage is that very few young artists, and very few of their supporters, can distinguish between the relatively and the absolutely good. To mistake the one for the other leads to unfounded assumptions: the artist gets stuck with himself, and with a limited idea of modernity, and his admirers in time take their bemusement elsewhere. Cruelty can result: it did no one any good to call Frank Dobson, in the 1920s, the best sculptor England had produced 'for about six hundred years'. To avoid misapprehensions of this sort an artist needs two things: friends and colleagues of real size, and an integrated idea of what is being done abroad. The carver's task does of course involve long periods of concentration, during which it may actually be harmful for him to become too involved with the outer world or too aware of what others are doing. Every large carving is an ordeal of steadiness and self-confidence,

38

36 Composition *Beechwood 13 in. 1932 Atlanta Art Museum, Georgia*

37 God of Fire, Xiuhtecutli, Huaxtec or Totonac civilization, Mexico *Sandstone 21 in. Musée de l'Homme, Paris*

and one way of getting through that ordeal is not to look up from the job in hand. But ideally this absorption should be balanced by an easy and pointful sociability at other times. Moore in the early 1930s had the benefit of a social context very different from that of his earlier years. His working conditions at that time were just about ideal: the balance between innocence and experience was more or less right, and he had for the first time the advantage of working as the friend and neighbour of people who were tunnelling in the same direction as himself.

By 'the balance between innocence and experience' I mean something quite specific. 'Experience' means an awareness of the ways in which sculpture had been emancipated since – well, since 1912, the year in which Boccioni had envisaged 'a complete renewal of this mummified art'. 'Innocence' means the capacity to let one's profoundest instincts override ideas taken ready-made from others. Experience without innocence leads to work that is feeble, imitative, and mannered; innocence without experience, to work that is provincial and unresonant. Just occasionally Moore had grazed the one, as in the awkward and inconclusive plaster *Relief* of 1931; just occasionally, in some of the naturalistic carvings of the same year, he had grazed the other. In the work with which we shall now deal both dangers were avoided.

This avoidance has a lot to do, as will be seen, with what was then called 'the modern movement'; but it also has something to do with Moore's own origins. I derided the use of the word 'miner' in connection with Moore's father; and it may seem illogical if, having outlawed it in relation to someone who had once worked in the pit, I use it in relation to someone who has been down the pit only as an observer in the 1940s. But Moore's is fundamentally an art of *burrowing*, and as the miner is pre-eminently a man who burrows I don't see how we can fail to make the connection, however lightly. Something in the inherited experience of the pit must be involved in Moore's lifelong preference for forms which have been opened out from within. (Just how strong that preference is, we may judge from the astonishment with which people received the *Standing Figure (Knife-edge)* of 1961.) Moore admits to enjoying the sensation of 'nibbling like a mouse'

at the interior of a block of wood or stone, but the metaphor of the miner at the pit-face is, surely, just as exact. And if Moore has never been tempted by the slender, aerial forms and the incorporeal structures which have preoccupied other sculptors we need look no further for the reason.

Moore began, then, with a basic predisposition towards massive forms that could be opened out from within. Where was he to go from there? The British Museum could prompt part of the way, and the Italian old masters likewise: but although Moore has always aimed at qualities which are both universal and timeless he has done so as an artist identified with his own time and with his own particular place in it. No artist who is any good can stand apart from the attitudes of his time, any more than by an effort of will he can reject the vocabulary of form which is current at that time. That vocabulary has a way of asserting itself at just the moment when an artist thinks to have got free of it. This is true of the Nabis' attempt to import the idiom of Japanese prints into French painting, and of the German Expressionists' borrowings from primitive art, and of every English painter's attempt to come to terms with Cézanne: what resulted is stamped inexpugnably with the date and the place of its origin.

So it is that, if some of Moore's early naturalistic carvings do not quite come off, even the novice can date them 'late 1920s'. Similarly, it is easy to spot points of resemblance between the more experimental pieces of that date and work which had been done, or was about to be done, overseas. But there is a great difference between an influence that is profoundly felt and an accidental likeness, due as much to the mere fact of contemporaneity as to any fundamental kinship.

If pressed, nowadays, to define his allegiances in 'the modern movement', Moore is likely to give a characteristically equable and simplified account in which everybody comes out well and there is no mention of the dilemmas in which he made the right choice. But the truth is, of course, that every artist has to make decisions all the time. If he makes the wrong ones, there's no disguising the fact. And Moore grew to maturity at a moment when it was impracticable to postpone those decisions. Today the repertory of living art is so wide, and

39 Composition *African wonderstone length 13 in.* 1933
Edward Wolfe, London

40 ALEXANDER ARCHIPENKO Struggle *Painted
plaster 23¾ in. 1914 Solomon R. Guggenheim Museum,
New York*

widely accepted, that an artist can go on
redistributing the ideas of others for a lifetime
without having to add anything much of his
own. But in 1932 nothing had caught on, in this
way: the *avant-garde* artist was in the position of
a man who might or might not tap a vein of
some unheard-of mineral, and in either case
was risking his life. Today he can go through
the same notions and risk no more than the man
who telephones to his broker and puts money
into I.C.I.

Duchamp-Villon, the sculptor-brother of
Marcel Duchamp and Jacques Villon, died in
1918. But in 1932 what he had said in 1915 was
still valid: 'We cannot fulfil the needs of art in
the idiom of bygone times. The things which we
want to embrace in sculpture are things with
which sculpture has never before been involved.
Which is right? Ourselves, or sculpture?'
Moore in his middle thirties had decided
opinions about the new idiom, and about the
ways in which people had tried to carry out
Duchamp-Villon's mandate. He regarded Brancusi, for instance, as someone whose historical
mission was now fulfilled.

Since the Gothic [Moore wrote in 1937], European
sculpture had been overgrown with moss, weeds –
all sorts of surface excrescences which completely
concealed shape. It has been Brancusi's special
mission to get rid of this undergrowth, and to make
us once again more shape-concious. To do this he
had to concentrate on very simple direct shapes, to
keep his structure, as it were, one-cylindered, to
refine and polish a single shape to a degree almost
too precious. . . . But it may no longer be necessary
to close down and restrict sculpture to the single
(static) form unit. We can now begin to open out,
to relate and combine together several forms of
varied sizes, sections and directions into one organic
whole.

The point could hardly have been put more
clearly. Remembering, too, the lack of fuss
which distinguishes Moore's carvings of the
middle and late 1930s, we could pick one of
Brancusi's own sayings: 'Simplicity is not a
thing to be aimed at. It is something one
arrives at in spite of oneself, as one draws near
to the real meaning of things.'

In his preference for forms that are massive
and full, Moore could count on an intuition
which Rodin had, but never followed through,

when he spoke of 'the human body conceived
as an urn, tapering to the waist, widening at the
hips, and forming a vase with an outline of
astonishing perfection – the amphora, which
holds in its flanks the life of the future. . . .'
Moore in the middle 1930s used over and over
again a form, half urn, half basket, which had
just these implications. Someone who had got
on to the ambiguity of near-human forms, and
who had always been splendidly radical in his
attitude to the future of sculpture, was Arp: and
in one or two pieces of *c.* 1932 Moore draws
near to the squidgy, all-purpose, sea-lion-like
forms of Arp (pls. 42, 43). Moore is not a whole-
hearted admirer of Arp, and I think that he
finds Arp's idiom too suave, too supple in a
slithery way, and too lacking in rugged incident.
Where the forms in Arp have an intrinsic
tension it is more, as he sees it, the tension of a
balloon blown tight than the tension of an
articulated structure in which rounded forms
press outward. But he is too fair-minded to
discount Arp's position as a man who has been
fundamentally on the right side since well
before 1914. Time and again, Arp's voice has
been heard in terms that Moore could echo:
'Bourgeois art is licensed lunacy. . . . It should
no longer be allowed to sully nature. Like the
early Christians, we must go back to essentials.'
And again: 'Art is a fruit born of man, just as
a fruit grows on a tree. But whereas all fruits
have forms that are intrinsically their own, the
human fruit which we call "art" nearly always
embodies an absurd resemblance to something
else. . . . I love nature, but not its substitutes.'
Arp pushed this belief to the point of wanting
his sculpture to merge into Nature and become
indistinguishable from it. But of course this has
never been the case; Arp's hand is unmistak-
able. And Moore likes, moreover, to get altogether closer to the origins of his imagery; to
worry them, in a word. But there will remain
certain kindred manifestations: among them,
the piece dated 1932 in which Arp set three
movable forms on one large form, and the
Concrétion Humaine of 1936.

Not much has been written about Moore's
contacts with the Surrealist movement. Most
English critics dislike Surrealism, dismiss it
almost *a priori*, and are embarrassed to think
that Moore was once involved with what seems
to them a whimsical and literary digression

41 Composition *Dark African wood 15¼ in. 1932 Sir
Kenneth Clark*

from the main purpose of art. It is true that a great deal of execrable work was done in the name of Surrealism, and it is also true that although England fathered several of Surrealism's ancestors (William Blake, Lewis Carroll, and Edward Lear) our contribution to the movement in its heyday has not always lasted very well. But Moore's sympathy with the movement was firm enough for him to contribute to the major Surrealist exhibitions which were held in 1936 in both London and New York. And even if he had not done so his sculptures of the 1930s would bear witness to the role played by Surrealism in liberating his imagination. For that imagination does, beyond a doubt, assert itself with a new boldness from about the time (in July 1930) when a new magazine, *Le Surréalisme au Service de la Révolution*, began to appear in Paris.

Moore was neither a whole-hearted Surrealist nor a convinced revolutionary, and he had no interest in either the para-literary conceits of Surrealism or the up-ended anecdotal paintings to which these gave rise. What moved him

profoundly, as it has continued ever since to move anyone with the slightest feeling for poetic statement in art, was the series of early works by Giacometti which were reproduced, sometimes with an accompanying text by the artist, in *Le Surréalisme au Service de la Révolution* and other reviews. More important even than certain physical parallels (see Giacometti's skeletal *Reclining Woman* of 1929 and his *Project for a Square*) was the attitude of mind which Giacometti defined in a famous essay in *Minotaure* in 1933.

Once the object [a generic name that he gave to all the sculptures of this period] is constructed I tend to see in it, metamorphosed and displaced, facts which have moved me deeply without my realizing it, and forms which I feel to be close to me – though (which makes them all the more disquieting) I often cannot identify them.

These lines could stand as the charter behind Moore's more enigmatic works in the 1930s. Moore has always worked in precisely this way – with facts that have moved him deeply without

2 Composition *African wonderstone* 17½ in. 1932
Tate Gallery, London

43 Composition *Carved concrete 24 in.* 1933 *British Council, London*

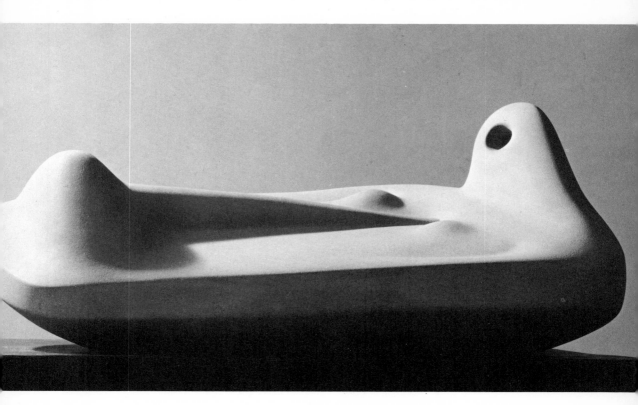

him realizing it, and forms which he feels to be close to him even if he cannot, and usually does not want to, identify them. Before 1931 his imagination was not free enough, nor his technique assured enough, to give them full scope: an exceptional excitement attaches, therefore, to the long series of works, many of them now unfamiliar to the English public, which he produced between 1931 and the outbreak of war in 1939.

One last environmental point. In the 1920s, as I have said, Moore had no companion of his own size. After 1939, he was of an age, and was working in an area of achievement, where artists no longer had close associates. But in the 1930s he did have, in Ben Nicholson and Barbara Hepworth, friends and neighbours who were close to him in age and in ambition. It would not do to exaggerate the intimacy which reigned, in working terms, between three artists, each of whom had a powerful individuality; Moore was essentially a thrusting and a solitary force. The inspired advocacy of Herbert Read soon put it about all over the world that a group of youngish artists was revitalizing British art; but although Moore enjoyed the friendliest of relations with his neighbours and was glad of

the advantages of a close-knit society (through Geoffrey Grigson, for instance, he came to know much of poets and poetry) he did not see art-life in terms of organization and campaigning. Many artists take a legitimate pleasure in the politics of art, and the 1930s were a great period for the manifesto and the statement of policy and the grouping and regrouping of like-minded individuals. Moore believes that people should be ready to fight for what they believe in, and he was a member of Unit One from 1933 onwards, and of the Seven and Five Society from 1934, just as he contributed to *Circle* in 1937. But whereas Paul Nash and Ben Nicholson regarded these activities as part of a holy war, Moore believed that the work would eventually make its own way and that political activity was tangential: valid and stimulating for some, dissipating and irrelevant for others.

Architecturally there is nothing special about Parkhill Road; socially it leans as much towards Kentish Town as towards Hampstead. No, 60, where Mondrian came to live in 1938, might be a trial run for a penitentiary, and the Mall Studios, in which Moore, Nicholson, Hepworth, and Herbert Read came to live five or six years earlier, have none of the grand

45 Figure *Corsehill stone 30 in.* 1933 *Carlo Ponti, Rome*

46 Reclining Figure *Carved reinforced concrete length
30½ in.* 1933 *Washington University, St Louis, Missouri*

Bohemianism of the London studios of late Victorian and Edwardian times. They are just cabins, a little apart from the life of London, in which people could get on with their work. Braque and Léger were occasional visitors; and after Hitler came to power, the original group were joined by Gabo, by Marcel Breuer, by Walter Gropius, and eventually by Mondrian; this did a great deal to de-provincialize what would have been, in any case, as powerful a concentration of younger talent as British art could show at that time. In 1933, Nicholson was thirty-nine, Moore thirty-five, Hepworth thirty: Hepworth had gone to Leeds School of Art at the age of seventeen and had therefore over-lapped with Moore both there and at the Royal College of Art, where both were students from 1921 until 1924. Like Moore, she went to Italy at the end of her time at the R.C.A.; and, again like Moore, she found that it was all she could do to adjust her Italian experience to the idea of sculpture which she had brought with her from her early days in Yorkshire and from her years as a student in London. She went,

however, at a substantially earlier phase in her development; and this is what she said later about it.

The Travelling Scholarship provided my most formative years by far. There had been something lacking in my childhood in Yorkshire, and that was *light.* In my early experience the sun never shone enough, the atmosphere rarely cleared, shadows were never sharp, surfaces never brilliant. Italy opened for me the wonderful realm of light – light which transforms and reveals, which intensifies the subtleties of form and contours and colour, and in which darkness – the darkness of window, door, or arch – is set as an altogether new and tangible object.

Read today, these remarks might seem to apply as much to drawings and reliefs made many years later by Ben Nicholson as to the naturalistic carvings of the human figure which Hepworth produced in her middle and late twenties. The key to much of Nicholson's grand-est work is in the architecture of the Ducal Palace at Urbino; but in the case of Hepworth

47 Figure *Travertine marble 16 in.* 1933 *H. Cady Wells,*   48 Family *Elmwood 36 in.* 1937–8 *Private Collection*
Santa Fé, New Mexico

Italian influence asserts itself above all in the lyrical ease and tenderness and fluency, so different from the basic awkwardness of so much English sculpture, of the carvings which she produced on her return from Italy. Looking at her Hoptonwood stone *Torso* of 1928 we at once remember Moore's clay *Torso* of 1925–6 (pl. 5), just as her ivory wood *Torso* of 1929 subtly echoes Moore's African wood *Torso* (pl. 20) of 1927. What is remarkable here is not that she should have followed the lead of an exceptionally powerful and substantially maturer personality, but that her contribution has already something that is her own.

Hepworth's original achievement as a sculptor can best be dated, however, from 1931. In 1930 she had seen paintings by Ben Nicholson for the first time, and as a result of this her work ceased to be concerned with an Anglo-Italian compromise: in her own words 'the exploration of free sculptural form' became its object. In carvings like the alabaster *Pierced Form* of 1931 and the green marble *Profile* of 1932 she was 'seeking a free assembly of certain formal elements, including space and calligraphy as well as weight and texture'. 'Space', here, may now be interpreted as putting a hole where no nineteenth-century sculptor would have thought of putting one, and 'calligraphy' as the notion of incising an otherwise flawless smooth surface. 'I had felt', she wrote later of the *Pierced Form*, 'the most intense pleasure in piercing the stone in order to make an abstract form and space'; and when she and Ben Nicholson visited Brancusi and Arp in 1932 she was able to go not as a sightseer but as someone with something to show. The two visits had above all a dis-inhibiting effect. In Brancusi's studio she got rid once and for all of the northern convention that sculpture is in some way 'fretted by the gravity of monuments to the dead'; and in the train on the way south to Avignon she 'stood in the corridor almost all the way looking out on to the superb Rhône Valley and thinking of the way Arp had fused landscape with the human form in so extraordinary a manner'. The instantaneous liberation indicated in these lines is as characteristic of Hepworth's nature and gifts as is the thorough-minded inner debate which has made Moore's career one of continual combat. The work itself did not become any easier, but the attitude of mind behind it became firmer easier, and more assured.

Both Moore and Hepworth were still, in fundamental terms, young people up from the provinces. People had been kind to them, but their conquests were their own, and they had started towards them from nothing at all. With Ben Nicholson the case was quite different. As the son of William and Mabel Nicholson and the nephew of James Pryde he had been born into the purple of the Edwardian art world. Every door in High Bohemia was open to his parents, and he might have evolved into one of those aimless, bereft, and insubstantial beings who go through life as 'So-and-so's son'. But as everyone knows, he didn't. Absenting himself from every milieu in which his parentage could have been of use to him, he set himself to excel in, and indeed to discover, an entirely different sort of painting. No one, in reality, is more delicately aware of the qualities of William Nicholson's painting; but to the outsider Ben Nicholson's career is one long act of rebellion against the upholstered art of Edwardian England.

At the time now under discussion, that rebellion was approaching one of its most decisive phases: Nicholson was shaping up for his first reliefs. The paintings done in France in 1932, during the journey which had so great an effect on Barbara Hepworth, include some of his most delicious and original creations: pictures in which he is manifestly having great fun with the apparatus of representation, looking back to Braque's up-tilted table-tops, looking forward to the jumps and contradictions of style which young painters were to discover in the 1960s, pitting one kind of statement against another, and counting as plus what had once been counted as minus – accidents and contradictions of texture. The 'free assembly of certain formal elements' of which Barbara Hepworth spoke was there already in these paintings.

Very broadly, therefore, one could say that 1932–3 was for all three artists a time of decision, during which they allied themselves once and for all with 'the modern movement' in Europe, and in particular with an activity that overran all the conventional frontiers. Nicholson's reliefs took something from sculpture; Moore and Hepworth raided calligraphy in many of their carvings. Idiom in both cases

52 Carving *Brown Hornton stone 20 in.* 1936 *Buchholz Gallery, New York*

53 Four-Piece Composition; Reclining Figure *Cumberland alabaster 20 in.* 1934 *Miss Lois Orswell, Narragansett, Rhode Island*

54 BARBARA HEPWORTH Two Forms *Blue Armenian marble 28 in.* 1933 *Graham Wigan Collection*

was exploratory, unprejudiced, epigrammatic, and free. Discussion and the interchange of ideas went on more or less continuously, and from April 1933 onwards the group had a gifted and tireless commentator in the person of Herbert Read, who had come to live only a yard or two away. While all this lasted – till the outbreak of war – Henry Moore was for the first and only time in contact with a coherent group of like-minded colleagues.

By 1932 Moore had discarded nearly all his naturalistic ambitions, but he did give them one last tremendous throw in the Sainsbury *Mother and Child* (pl. 35). This has the alertness, the emotional tension, of the early Pre-Colombian influence. It has the shifts and anomalies of scale which had begun in the previous year. It has the variety of axes which allows the sculptor to shift the interest continually within a basically simple design. And it has the swelling-from-within which Moore had developed in, for instance, the Clark *Composition* (pl. 41) of dark African wood in the same year. Here the shoulder, elsewhere the knees and the breast, were

the points at which Moore was managing to give his carvings a new counter-movement, an expansion from within outwards, that was the very reverse of the tightened, constricted block-hugging movement of 1924–5.

This was the last occasion for ten years and more on which Moore was to show identifiable human beings in an identifiable situation. The pull of pure sculptural invention was strengthened around this time by the example of continental colleagues, and the human component in his sculptures began to be treated in an ever more radical way. Occasional echoes of recent paintings by Picasso, or of sculpture by Archipenko, or of Pre-Colombian art, do not effect here or elsewhere, the basic individuality of Moore's work. One or two pieces (notably the Tate *Composition* of 1932 in African wonder stone, pl. 42) reflected a wish to adapt the formal language of Arp to purely human preoccupations. A piece like the British Council's *Composition* of 1933 (pl. 43) is like a comment again, on Rodin's view of the urn and the amphora as metaphors for the human body

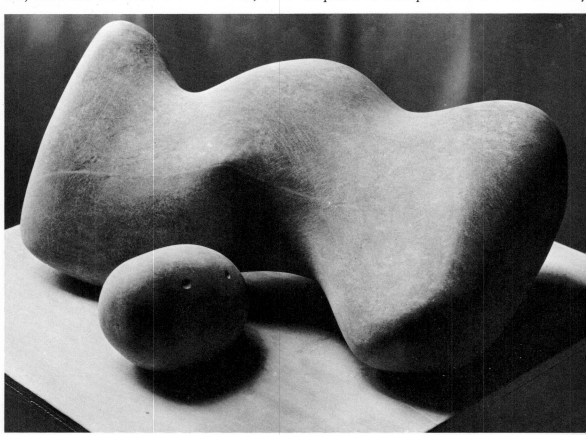

But Moore was pushing out – literally, in some cases – towards formal inventions which had nothing to do with anyone but himself. Two examples of this are the figures carved in Corsehill stone; time has conferred a strange immunity on these mysterious works. Faced, for instance, with the *Figure* of 1933–4 (pl. 45) and even more so with *Reclining Figure* of a year later (pl. 44) it would be difficult for anyone not forewarned to name their date, origins, and function. The *Figure* is the apotheosis of the swelling, outward-thrusting movement on which Moore had been working. It is a piece in which the swelling *is* the subject, to a degree not paralleled elsewhere, and all other themes and incidents are subordinated to it. There is no trace, in this figure, of the violated block: all accords with the mysterious, even, powerful and yet perfectly contained swelling of the stone, which seems, however irrationally, to have been modelled from within. In the colossal strength of throat, neck, back, shoulders, and breast, the figure also looks forward to the more than life-size figures of the late 1950s. The *Reclining Figure*

is, on the other hand, an isolated and hermetic piece to which nothing in the later work corresponds. At once bather and bath, coffin and swathed corpse, Libyan sand-formation and early racing motor-car complete with helmeted driver, it belongs to past, present, and future impartially.

In 1933, when working for his second show at the Leicester Galleries, Moore turned to carved and reinforced concrete for a *Reclining Figure* (pl. 46) now in the Washington University, St Louis, which harked back to the strutted, opened-out structure of the Zimmerman figure, made use of incised lines to focus certain points of interest, and for the arms and legs exploited thinnesses impossible in stone. Adrian Stokes was the first to see that this seemingly ruthless refashioning of the human frame was not, as it seemed to many, a complete violation of the European tradition.

Here [he wrote] are the peaks of the feminine form, realized at last freely, with the aid of mere connecting rods; here as twin summits stand the tall

56 Carving *Blue Ancaster stone 16 in. 1934 Artist's Collection*

58 Carving *Travertine marble 18 in. 1936 Private Collection*

57 Square Form *Brown Hornton stone 21 in. 1936 Artist's Collection*

59 Reclining Figure *Hoptonwood stone length 33 in.* 1937 *Miss Lois Orswell, Narragansett, Rhode Island*

60 Sculpture *Hoptonwood stone 20 in.* 1937 *Artist's Collection*

cylindrical knees; here as dolmens are the breasts; here the topmost plateau of the head; while so uniform and simple are the links between these forms that the composition as a whole may suggest an image of Cleopatra reclining in the stern of an Egyptian barge, her long body in such unison with the boat that her propped-up head, as though the topmost section of a rudder oar, guides, steers, and governs. . . .

Many artists, having struck a vein of effort which could call forth so apt and so poetical a tribute, would have kept on at it. But 1933 was not, in fact a very fertile year for Moore (the Sylvester catalogue notes only six items) and the pieces that he did get down to were quite different in character. Some of them had to do with the new dynamic element of the hole (pl. 47). One (S137) has striking parallels with the Barbara Hepworth grey alabaster *Figure* (1933): but the differences (his shoulder-form thrust out from within, hers tenderly smoothed down into place) are as striking as the likenesses. In one little-known piece, the African wonderstone *Composition* (pl. 42), Moore effected a compromise or middle-ground between the opened-out forms of the St Louis *Reclining Figure* and the closed, fortress-like forms towards which he was also tending. This piece serves, in fact, as a marker-buoy for today's student, who can steer by the flattened oval of the hole, the face-form held over from the *Double Head* of 1928, and the new sophistication in Moore's handling of areas which in former days might have been left more or less as the block provided them.

The point is that at this stage in his development idea and execution were one; the hesitations of the 1920s were gone for ever. If his early pieces are occasionally cryptic, it is because the idea has not quite been dragged out of the block: but from 1933 onwards if a piece is cryptic it is because it is meant to be so. The female human body was still Moore's chief subject, but henceforward it is not merely opened up, but broken first into two pieces, then into four. It was also closed down, on occasion, into an object, at first sight inscrutable, which revealed on inspection all the attributes of the human frame. It was slotted, grooved, hollowed out, shored up, incised, and knobbed.

61 Two Forms *Ironstone 7¼ in. 1934 Marlborough*
Fine Art

62 Two Forms *African wood length 21 in. 1934 Museum of Modern Art, New York*

These mysterious carvings are among Moore's most substantial and enduring contributions to living art. But it would be naïve to suppose that they did not draw to a limited extent on an idiom that was already in the air. Moore has none of the mischief, and still less of the whimsicality, of Arp's reliefs, that delight some people and exasperate others; but a relief like Arp's *Torso with Flower Head* of 1924 opens up a mode of expression that both Moore and Hepworth were to carry several stages further. Nor do the jokey titles of works like Arp's *Head with Annoying Objects* (1930) obscure the fact that these were pioneer attempts to make sculptures in several movable pieces which would hold up as absolute works of art.

Potent, also, was the anti-rational imagery of European Surrealism. In a Dali or a Tanguy of 1929 the forms may look totally wilful; but if we break them down objectively an element of unconscious conformity can often be detected – and what they conform to is an idea of closed-or-open form that reappears four and five years later in Moore and Hepworth. What we are talking about is not the deliberate appropriation by one artist of another's formal vocabulary: it is the universal presence of forms which belong to a particular moment in the history of art and force themselves upon artists whose conscious intentions have nothing in common. Nothing could be further from the aspirations of Parkhill Road than a painting like Dali's *Birth of Liquid Desires* (1932) (pl. 49), but the foreground form is, none the less, midway between Arp's reliefs of the 1920s and certain pierced and tunnelled forms in Moore. The metamorphoses to which the human body is subject in Moore's figures of the 1930s could never have come about in quite the same way if the arbitrary revision of natural form had not been one of the fundamentals of Surrealism. It cannot be quite coincidental, for example, that in May 1933 *Le Surréalisme au Service de la Révolution* published an illustrated article by Tanguy in which re-invented objects turn out to be related sometimes to human, sometimes to botanical, sometimes to mineral form. Re-invention was in the air: once again, it cannot be altogether an

63 Sculpture *White marble 22 in.* 1935 *Joel Starrels Collection, Chicago*

accident that 1936, a year of outstanding importance to Moore's *œuvre*, was marked also by the Exhibition of Surrealist Objects at the house of Charles Ratton in the rue de Marignan in Paris. Those who did not actually see this show, which appears to have run for a week only, could pick up many of its ideas from a special issue of *Cahiers d'Art* in which were illustrated (I quote from Marcel Jean's *History of Surrealist Painting*) 'stibnites from Transylvania which looked like hedgehogs, a lump of bismuth of which the surface looked to have been set up in printing-type, limonites that had the look of exotic tubers, and a calcite formation that looked just like a snowman'. Equally potent at this time was the idea of the 'perturbed object', typified by the household objects which had been completely transmogrified by the eruption of Mont Pelé, in Martinique, in 1902: any number of analogies could be found between the frantic deformations to which these had been subjected and the revision of the human body, for expressive purposes, of which Picasso was later the pioneer.

This was the heyday also of the interpreted object: the pebble or rock structure which could be grouped, incised, painted, or rearranged to make an unexpected and poetical impact. This was the year, finally, in which Max Ernst came upon the mathematical constructions in the Institut Henri Poincaré which were then photographed for *Cahiers d'Art* by Man Ray. In these constructions, the formulae of space geometry were put into concrete form. For generations they had fulfilled merely a specific didactic function. But then, on the intervention of a major artist, they suddenly assumed a whole range of auxiliary meanings and gave added authority to researches which had got under way quite independently. Once again, it might be too much to trace a direct line between this incident and the activities of Parkhill Road. But, as will shortly be seen Moore drew a year or two later on comparable constructions in the Science Museum in London which he had known since student days: Henrici's (1876) visualizations of algebraic formulae added something, beyond a

64 Four Forms *African wonderstone 22 in.* 1936 *Henry Hope Collection*

65 Two Forms *Hornton stone 16 in.* 1936 *Artist's Collection*

66 Head *Elmwood and string 8 in.* 1938 *Marlborough Fine Art, New York*

doubt, to the vocabulary of Moore in the late 1930s.

Above all, Picasso had proved by the end of 1930 that the human figure, broken up and remade in radical style, could manifest a heightened expressiveness. Picasso's heavy-limbed neo-Classical figures of 1920–2 lie behind the St Louis *Reclining Figure* (pl. 46) of 1932, just as the aggressive distortions and enclosed hollow spaces of Picasso's *Seated Bather* of 1930 clearly prefigure elements in later reclining figures by Moore. But the message as received in Parkhill Road was not 'Do it like this!': it was 'Go ahead!' Ben Nicholson once said to me, 'Courage is the first thing I think of when I think of Picasso': and what Picasso did at this time was to give courage to people who lacked it, and to reinforce it when they had it already.

Moore went ahead, therefore, with redoubled energy: and that energy multiplied within itself instead of being spread laterally over a wide area. I would rank very high in his *œuvre* pieces like the shoe-like African wonderstone *Reclining Figure* of 1934 and the two-, three-, and four-piece compositions of the same year. Once again, an instructive comparison can be drawn between the African wonderstone figure and a Barbara Hepworth of the previous year, the *Reclining Figure* in white alabaster. Of the two, the Hepworth keeps closer to the facts of human anatomy: shoulder, pelvis, head, and hip vary mainly in scale from the *données* of Nature, even if the clog-form of the whole is clearly marked '1933'. The Moore, by contrast, is the first in a series that extends over the years 1934–7 and grows progressively more enigmatic. In carvings like the *Square Form* (pl. 51) of 1934 Moore sometimes ran parallel to paintings and reliefs of the period by Nicholson; but in such cases the circles and the rectangular incisions occurred unexpectedly on the flanks, or on the topmost surfaces, of monumental and disquieting structures in which were fused all the things that Moore had learned from the past and all the things that he had learned from the present, and from his own instinctual drives. Moore *is* Moore, in these pieces, with an intensity not excelled anywhere in his work.

Moore's art at its best is, to my mind, an inclusive art. It allows, that is to say, of the inclusion of elements which in another artist's work might seem incongruous or mutually

68 Stringed Figure no. 4 *Lignum vitae and string 14 in.*
1938 *G. Burt Collection*

69 Mother and Child *Lead and wire 7¼ in.* 1939
Rodney Phillips Collection

70 Reclining Figure *Elmwood 42 in.* 1936 *City Art
Gallery, Wakefield*

contradictory, and is the stronger for thei
presence. In a Barbara Hepworth like th
alabaster *Two Forms With Sphere* of 1934 or th
white marble *Two Forms* of the following year w
see, by contrast, an exclusive art: an art which
like Brancusi's, proceeds by excluding what i
irrelevant to the formal proposition that is bein
stated. All gross matter is purged; what remain
has an absolute purity and an ideal simplicit
of statement. In Moore's pieces of the same dat
the experience on offer is radically different. I
the Hepworths are sacred places, the Moore
are architectural environments long worn an
weathered by human use. There are shifts c
idiom and scale, deliberate antitheses of weigh
and proportion, points of high drama an
points of repose. The whole bent and characte
of a piece like Moore's destroyed *Three Forms* c
1934 varied according to the place and th
angle from which it was looked at: Moore wa
all the time *adding*, that is to say, taking in mor
and more potential experiences and gettin
them to live together, where a Brancusi or
Hepworth would have subtracted and gone o
subtracting till the final piece offered one singl
experience that was, in intention, the sum of al
other possible experiences. But Moore himsel
defined his attitude when, not long ago, he sai
roundly that 'Great sculpture is not abou
perfection.'

The notion of inclusiveness, in Moore
applied also to other aspects of his work. In th
1920s his sculptures had to do, broadly speaking
with the cross-breeding of direct observation o
the human figure with inferences drawn eithe
from 'primitive' or from Italian sources. From
about 1931 onwards he began to admit source
material of quite another kind. This was due i
part to the example of continental Surrealism
and in part to the notion, then newly formed
that anything can be the point of departure fo
a work of art if it is made use of in the right way
This notion has been of cardinal importance to
Moore's work ever since: it first got under way
in the drawn studies of bone-form, dated 1932
and in sculptures dated 1934 which are really
found-and-altered objects in the pure tradition
of continental Surrealism. The notion of the
accidental in art, and of the object found and
altered, is taken for granted in post-war paint
ing and sculpture, but in the early 1930s i
came as an immense revelation. Paul Nash a

71 Reclining Figure *Elmwood 42 in.* 1936 *City Art Gallery, Wakefield*

that time was a neighbour and friend of the Parkhill Road group, and no one was quicker than he, in paintings like *Earth Home* or *Landscape of the Megaliths*, to grasp what it meant to form an alliance with prehistory. What Adrian Stokes called 'the lapsed movement of the centuries' turned out to be on the side of living art; and Henry Moore began to work on meteoric stones at just the time when Giacometti and Max Ernst were hauling huge boulders from the bed of a glacier in the Engadine. With increasing years and increasing confidence he has begun to turn the tables on Nature; it is a curious fact about the glade which he uses as a mortuary for old plasters that the tree-forms which mark its boundaries do on occasion echo earlier sculptures by Moore. But in the 1930s, when living art was still the concern of an isolated few, there was reassurance in the idea that what seemed to many people outrageous and wilful practices were paralleled by phenomena which predated the very notion of art. And, concurrently, the everyday world was revising all our ideas of scale and 'importance'. Nobody, for instance, was more whole-heartedly a man of the present than Fernand Léger, and it would never have occurred to him to enlist prehistory as his ally. But he knew what was happening to the nature of imagery in art. 'A quite novel poetry,' he said, 'the poetry of the *transformed object*, is coming into the world, and a new art will be built up on these new discoveries, this new truth.' The object could, of course, be transformed in innumerable ways; and one of them was exemplified by the re-invented forms with which Henry Moore was working all through the 1930s.

Among these, the closed and cryptic forms to which I have already referred have few parallels in Moore's later work. The sculptures in two, three, or four pieces have, on the other hand, their counterpart in many large post-war sculptures. Some observers have likened them to pieces by Giacometti, dated 1931, but even if the initial push may have come from this direction Moore rapidly made the idea his own. Nothing could be more characteristic of him

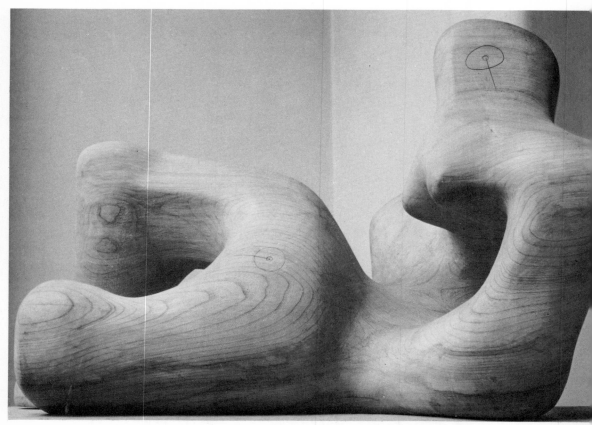

72 Stringed Reclining Figure *Bronze length 11 in.*
1939 *Private Collection*

73 Reclining Figure *Green Hornton stone length 55 in.*
1938 *Tate Gallery, London*

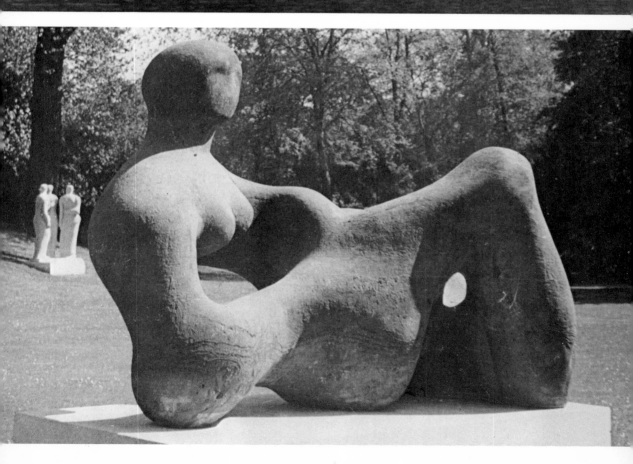

74 and 75 Reclining Figure *Elmwood length 6 ft. 9 in.*
1939 *Onslow Ford Collection*

for instance, than the *Two Forms* in Pynkado
wood of 1934 (pl. 62). The basic formal idea,
here, is that of the sheltering mother: part
shoulder, part pelvis, the larger form bends
over and nurtures the other in just the attitude
that would earlier have served a naturalistic
end, and was later carried over into the *Reclining
Mother and Child* of 1960–1 (pl. 193). The monumental two- and three-piece Reclining Figures
of the early 1960s are not so far, for that matter,
from the *Four-piece Composition: Reclining Figure*
of 1934. Moore was still working as much as
possible on the principle of the altered object,
and in the 1934 piece there are traces of
Surrealist idiom which later gave place to
altogether more magniloquent procedures. But
the fundamental idea is there: that of breaking
up the human body to make an image that was
truly three-dimensional and could be explored
exhaustively from every angle. After completing
an experimental four-part piece in 1936 Moore
seems, however, to have laid the idea aside for
the best part of twenty-five years.

It was not the only idea to be so treated. The
white marble *Sculpture* of 1935 (pl. 63) looked
till recently like an isolated attempt with
material which, more than any other, had
emotional connotations for the layman. For
how many generations was it not accepted that
a sculpture which was not in white marble was
not really a sculpture at all? Cathedral and
cemetery alike bear out the belief, and the
sculptor is rare who is not in some way conditioned by the built-in suavity of the material.
By cutting into the block and creating an effect
of deep shadow and architectural contrast
Moore was able to beat off the dangers of
sentimentality: and, thirty years later, the
formal idea of this piece was revived, toughened
and given an unforced majesty in the *Archer* of
1965 (pl. 212). In bronze, this is one of the most
cogent of Moore's later works; but in the dead
white cast which was prepared for *Homage to
T.S. Eliot* at the Globe Theatre in June 1965
made an impression of other-worldly magnifi-
cence. Somewhere within every member of the
audience there stirred the ancient idea of white
as the embodiment of all that is grandest and

76 Reclining Figure *Lead length 12 in.* 1939 *Victoria and Albert Museum, London*

most solemn in human experience: that Moore could in this way renew an idea long dragged in the dust was one more proof of his stature.

An idea characteristic of the later 1930s, and not renewed since, is that of the stringed figure. Moore developed this while exploring the notion of the opened-out, as opposed to the closed and hermetic, figure. The initial idea came from didactic models (pl. 50) in the Science Museum, London, and in 1937 Moore produced a *String Relief* which is basically a Surrealist interpretation of the human body with string drawn taut between one and another of the three components. David Sylvester defined the threefold function of the string as follows:

It contrasts, in its tautness, with the curvilinear contours of the mass. It establishes a barrier between the space enclosed by the sculpture's mass and the space which surrounds the sculpture – only a barrier which, being a cage and not a wall, can contain the space on its open side while allowing it to remain visible. Above all, the string provokes movement of the spectator's eye along its length and thereby increases his awareness of the space

within the sculpture – especially when, as in t *Bird Basket* of 1939, one set of taut strings can seen through another, so creating a counterpoi of movement which brings to life the space arou and within which the strings operate.

The stringed element was used in 1938–9 emphasize and define the openness of abstra sculptures which were, in effect, standing figur or Mothers and Children under another nan (pl. 68). Eventually one of them was flat called *Mother and Child* (pl. 69), and in the san year, 1939, a *Stringed Reclining Figure* made th point even clearer. Moore's formal experimen have always been made, in the last resort, in th interests of some new exploration of the huma figure, and in the Reclining Figure in questic the string contrasts with the easy, wave-lik movement of the rest of the piece and lite ally pulls together what would otherwise be group of disconnected episodes.

In so far as Moore was widely known at th outbreak of war, he was known for his majo Reclining Figures: and in this country abov all for the one (pl. 73) bought by the Tat

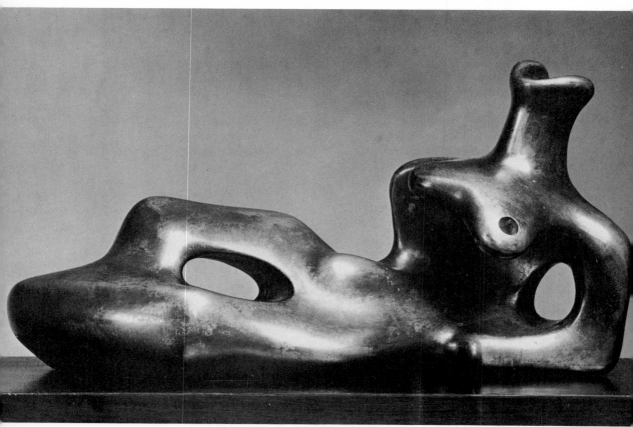

Reclining Figure *Lead length 14 in.* 1938 *Museum
Modern Art, New York*

allery in 1939, shortly after John Rothenstein
came Director. This differs from his earlier
clining figures in that the inspiration of
imitive art has given place to the inspiration
landscape; and, in particular, of the rolling,
ndulatory, and predominantly pacific land-
ape of England. Not the Alps, but downland;
ot the fjord, but the Seven Sisters; not the
oraine, but the moors – these would define,
ithin the limits of language, the tone of
Ioore's human landscape. The mountains
ove Carrara are to this day a holy place in
Ioore's eyes, but I doubt if it would occur to
im to take them bodily into his work, whereas
ith the broody, unemphatic, heavy-shouldered
ar-mountains of England he feels free to
anœuvre as he pleases.

The 1939 pieces have in common, also, a
ew homogeneity of idiom. An incision or two
n the Wakefield piece of 1936 (pl. 71) may
ok back a year or two, and the enormous
ubbed right foot harks back to the late 1920s.
ut in general the 1939 pieces get clear away
om the jumps and incongruities of Surrealist
idiom: clear away, too, from the note of panicky
awareness which was part of the Mexican
legacy. The whole body now speaks, instead of
the eyes or the set of the head. The auxiliary
hole is much in evidence, adding an echo to the
caverns and tunnels which Nature has provided. The body's own axes are countered by
others inherent in the sculpture itself; and to
vacancies not in Nature Moore has joined links
and embankments and great swooping, swing-
ing formal gestures for which there is, once
again, no warrant in our anatomy. In the
Onslow-Ford figure not only the chest but the
head, the breast, and several re-invented areas
are pierced, so that the piece echoes along all
its length with tunnels and entrances. But all
four pieces demonstrated an idea formulated by
Moore himself: that 'sculpture in air is possible,
where the stone contains only the hole, which is
the intended and considered form'.

Architecture played a part, also, when Moore
incorporated the notion of an arch within the
notion of a hill. And if we remember the
awkwardnesses and incongruities of the work

78, 79 and 80 Figures from different periods:
Reclining Figure *Lead length 11¾ in. 1938 Victoria and Albert Museum, London*

Reclining Figure *Carved reinforced concrete length 43 in. 1932 CAM Collection, St Louis*

Draped Reclining Figure *Bronze length 6½ in.* 1956
Private Collection

done in the 1920s we shall see at once that in these four pieces the pressures, outward and inward, are in perfect equilibrium. Moore has both respected and fought against the material's own nature. And the sculpture is opened out not merely in a physical sense but morally also, in that nothing is hidden away, counterfeited, or protected by the block. No one can gainsay, in this context, the virtuosity of the Onslow-Ford figure; but the other three seem to me superior, because Moore went all out to establish, not a chain of holes, but one single hole so large, so complete, so obviously 'important', that it became the sculpture's principal subject. Initially he did it in elmwood, a material unpopular with some because of its powerful, coffin-recalling smell, but a great favourite with Moore. Two years later he brought it off in the less tractable medium of green Hornton stone: the Tate *Reclining Figure* (pl. 73) is one of the grandest of all Moore's achievements, and it would form an ideal full close to this chapter, before the artificial close enforced by the outbreak of war, if it were not that in the six small

Reclining Figures dated 1939, which measure between five and thirteen inches apiece, there are ideas which, as we shall see, he took up again on a larger scale in the 1950s.

81 Drawing from life *Wash 22 in. × 15 in.* 1928
Mrs Irina Moore

IV 1939-1945

Moore had always made drawings, and even where they seem least related to his mature work in sculpture they often turn out in the end to have a kinship the stronger, perhaps, for remaining so long a secret. In the Tate *Reclining Figure*, for instance, which has just been discussed, there are echoes of more than one of the seated life drawings of 1928: that majestic poise of the head did not have to be invented.

Life-drawing, Moore said recently, 'is the most exacting form of concentrated activity that exists. Carving is like digging up the garden by comparison.' The relationship between drawing and sculpture is, moreover, one of the aspects of his work about which Moore allows himself a certain degree of self-consciousness. He knows that for a young artist whose sculptures may take weeks or even months to complete there is a valuable freedom in the ability to make a drawing in an hour or so, if necessary by artificial light, and without the feeling that a false move may be fatal, as it may be in the case of a carving. He can even afford to work, as Moore did sometimes in the 1930s, in quasi-unthinking style, allowing the instinct of the moment to guide his hand. He can grope around among ideas that he may never want to carry further,

and if he is a sculptor he can invent natural or architectural settings for his work and see how it stands up to them.

These are examples of creative drawing. Some sculptors, by contrast, turn out drawings which are no better than souvenirs of their sculptures, and there are others whose draughtsmanship is so feeble as to make one wonder that they ever let the sheets out of the studio. With Moore, the worked-up 'exhibition drawing' is rare, and in nearly every case his drawings are genuine explorations of ideas. This was the case, especially, in the 1930s, when he was constantly running on ahead in his drawings and trying out ideas which for technical and other reasons he was not yet ready to put into sculpture. One instance already quoted is that of the Bone-drawings of 1933; another, the drawings for strutted reclining figures, dated 1931, which were well ahead of the strutted sculpture of that kind which is now in St Louis; a third, the drawings (1936) of sculpture against a wall; a fourth, the coloured drawing of 1939 in which the idea of the internal and external form was first demonstrated.

But as far as Moore's popularity was concerned, the most pregnant of all the drawings of

MOORE

82 Standing Figure, drawn from life *Chalk and pen*
7 in. × 8 in. 1926 *Miss Mary Moore*

83 Figures in a cave *Chalk and wash 15 in. × 22 in.*
1936 J. A. Paton Walker (British Council, London)

he 1930s was the *Figures in a cave* of 1936 (pl. 3). Moore did not often define the space in which his figures appeared: more commonly they perched in mid-page and with no attempt at localization. But here for once were human beings wearing ankle-length robes in what was unmistakably a cave. Now the symbolic cave or Virgilian *antrum* has always played a large part in Moore's idiom, but this was the first time that an inhabited cave had been treated naturalistically. It had no successors, though from time to time projects for sculpture were set in a cabin-like environment from which claustrophobia was never far absent. In the spring of 1940 Moore produced, too, a whole group of ideas for Sculpture, in which figures were piled one on top of another, heaped in a shallow picture-space and against a background which, when defined at all, was dark and prison-like. In the autumn of the same year life caught up with art when Moore, as an Official War Artist, began to study the underground shelters, and in particular the shelters improvised in the Underground, where thousands of people passed the night at the time of the Blitz. The drawings which resulted were made from memory, not on the spot, and they have as much a visionary as a documentary significance. Moore was spellbound by the fact that these thousands of people were lying helpless, deep in the earth, while things were done to them. The dreadful passivity of the scene was what lingered in his mind, and when he came to make the drawings the people in them looked as if each had a winding-sheet, not a blanket. Seen in close-up, individual heads were nearer to Géricault's mortuary studies for the *Radeau de la Méduse*, or to Giacometti's sculpture of a dying man (*Head on a Stalk*, 1947), than to the stylized cheerfulness which was current form at the time and did, in reality, survive in even the most gruesome conditions. As a document of the times the Shelter drawings strike me as haunting but incomplete. They bring out the nightmarish, slave-ship quality which Moore can so well evoke to this day in conversation, and in some of the more crowded scenes there is even a foretaste of what Belsen and Buchenwald

84 Page from Shelter Sketchbook *Chalk, pen and watercolour* 1941 *Mrs Irina Moore*

85 Page from Shelter Sketchbook *Chalk, pen and watercolour* 1941 *Mrs Irina Moore*

would look like on the day of liberation. The drawings are unforgettable; but their unforgettableness does not spring from the nature of the scene portrayed. It springs from the alliance of certain elements in that scene with certain basic preoccupations in Moore. For what is man, in these drawings, but a burrowing animal, far from the surface, filled with strange terrors, weirdly accoutred and uneasily reclining? What had been exceptional – a private nightmare – was suddenly the lot of everyone: to poses and postures which had been prompted by the instincts of art there was suddenly no alternative. (In one shelter drawing, for instance (pl. 85), nature fell in with art as one of the sleepers raised her right leg in precisely the posture which Moore has used over and over again in his reclining figures.) History put in Moore's way precisely those images of envelopment and protectiveness which had been thrust on him in earlier years by the shape of the block, or by tendencies implicit in art history, or by his own unconscious memories. People lived out, on the platform of the Underground, rituals normally reserved for the healing quiet of the hearth; and if Moore, in these drawings, is nowhere concerned with circumstantial detail of the kind which at the time made the whole thing bearable, he managed to hoist a petty and comfortless existence on to the level of symbolic adventure.

With the Shelter drawings, Moore became what he has been ever since: one of the keepers of the public conscience. People were persuaded, when they saw these drawings, that a certain dogged grandeur attached to the life they were leading. The squalid and self-preservatory elements in that life dropped away, and what remained behind was on the scale of epic. (What epic, after all, is without its *longueurs*?) And as Moore is not at all a hermetic or cerebral artist there is no doubt that he, likewise, was sustained and encouraged by this sudden contact with a large public. It came at the right moment: teaching had come to an end with the outbreak of war, it was out of the question to get a man-size block of stone or a chunk of the right sort of tree, his London studio was damaged by bombing, and his exhibition at the Leicester Galleries in 1940 was to be the last for five years. It was a difficult time.

The Shelter drawings were followed in 1942 by a series of drawings of miners at the coal-face. Once again the motif of burrowing, the claustrophobic shallowness of the picture-space and the primary activity of the bent and twisted human body were ideally adjusted to the idiom but as most people prefer to avert their attention from the realities of the coal-face these drawings have never enjoyed anything like the popularity of the others. But there is very little else in Moore's work to compare with them for directness and intensity of observation – or, for that matter, for power and economy of design. And when the whiteness of a human body is coaxed forth from the environing dark, there comes to mind Moore's favourite among the draughtsmen of the last hundred years: Seurat.

Between 1940 and 1943 there is nothing at all in the way of sculpture in the Sylvester catalogue. Large worked-up drawings alone mark the period; but they mark it in ways which now seem to have a note of prophecy. Nothing came, admittedly, of the projects in which whole groups of figures were disposed in an enclosed area, half-palace, half-prison, as if waiting around for some classic drama to get under way. Nor did anything follow from that last fling of the Surrealist in Moore, the *Crowd looking at a tied-up object* of 1942: but this is in its own right one of the most haunting and enigmatic of his inventions. (Watching, in later years, Moore's Upright Motives being swathed in readiness for a journey, a visitor to his studio could remember this drawing and find it re-enacted exactly before him.)

A drawing like the *Crowd looking at a tied-up object* prompts the idea, so often mooted by admirers of Moore, that he should have worked for the stage. Invitations to design scenery for Wagner's *Ring*, and for *King Lear*, and for one or two heavyweight theatrical ventures, did in fact come his way, but he always refused them. During the war, when sculpture was a practical impossibility, he might have been open to the idea, but in normal times he has always dreaded the interruptions which anything of the sort would entail.

I was frightened of it. If I got my coat-tails into the mangle of the theatre I'd be drawn in bodily. The first thing I should do would not be as good as I should like it to be, and I'd have to try again to prove that I could really do it, or to find out what

Tilbury Shelter. Page from Shelter Sketchbook
alk, pen and watercolour 1941 *Mrs Irina Moore*

Women & children with bundles. List of subjects for
shelter drawings –
1 View from inside shelter at
night time, with moonlight & flare
light on bombed buildings.
② Two half figures in closed-in space
with opening showing burning
building outside.
3. Single figure against shell splintered
wall.
4. Head in a shelter – head in a box
closed in.
5 Figures wrapped in blankets.
6 Figure in a bombed street.

Tilbury shelter

Figures showing faces lit up – rest
...ies in silhouette.
...is lying against platform with great bales of paper above also making
...ambulators with bundles.
...Dramatic, dismal lit, masses of reclining figures fading to perspective
...nt — Scribbles & scratches, chaotic foreground. Chains hanging from
...crane.
...& woman in bathchair. Bearded jews blanketed sleeping in deck
...scars Tunnel (bundles of old clothes that are people)   chairs
...nks with women feeding children
...rk wet settings (entrance to Tilbury)
...en with shawls to keep off draughts, women wearing handkerchiefs on heads
...nk & rubbish & chaotic untidiness around

87 Falling buildings. Page from Shelter Sketchbook
Chalk, pen and watercolour 1949 *Mrs Irina Moore*

88 Morning after an air-raid. Page from Shelter
Sketchbook *Chalk, pen and watercolour* 1941 *Mrs Irina
Moore*

89 Moore as War Artist sketching in a Yorkshire coal-mine, 1942 *Barnet Saidman*

90 Studies of miners at work *Chalk, pen and watercolour* 1942 *Birmingham Art Gallery*

was wrong the first time, and so on. Sculpture takes up so much of one's time, and it would be the simplest thing in the world to have one's energies dissipated in other ways.

But I think that the fundamental answer is that in Moore's best sculptures idea and action are one, whereas in a stage-set, however distinguished, action has to be added to idea. A great figure by Moore doesn't have to move, or talk, or do anything to round off and fulfil its existence. It *is* drama: condensed, caught up, concentrated. But in wartime, when figures of this kind could not be made, Moore did experiment with what were, in effect, stage-settings; and after the war – sometimes ten or more years later – he realized some of these notions in bronze. In 1952, for instance, he wrapped two figures round the outer edge of a right-angled projection which jutted out, as if into the middle of a stage. Sometimes the human figure was seated, in 1956–7, against a wall, or on a flight of steps, as if in the open-air theatre of the Greeks. A year or more later, 'motives' of a

quasi-animal sort were set in front of a wa into which rectangular openings had been le Eventually, in 1962, the cycle was complete and the wall itself became the whole subject the sculpture.

In all this, the polarity of Moore the sculpte and Moore the draughtsman is made unusual clear. As if in some classic textbook of war, tw possible attitudes are exemplified and mac visible: the one darting ahead on reconnai sance, the other trundling behind with th heavy equipment that wins the final battl Poring over the wartime drawings, we som times find a detailed forecast of a sculptur which would be carried out as soon as coi ditions allowed: a sheet of 1942, for exampl foretells exactly the look of one of Moore noblest reclining figures, the Cranbrook Aca demy elmwood figure (pl. 102) of 1945–6. I others, a naturalistic drawing of the female nud appears side by side with intermediary sketche in which that nude is partly opened up, part] left as it is in life. Long after Moore had cease to go to either shelter or mine, certain figure

91 At the coal-face *Chalk, pen, wash and watercolour*
13 in. × *22 in.* 1942 *Whitworth Art Gallery, Manchester*

were enclosed in coffin-like areas which derive from the experience of Underground and coal-face. Some of these were later worked up as sculptures, but there are others which got no further: notably a very curious invention of 1944, which looks like a double-bass half in and half out of its case. There are indications, too, of the preoccupation with drapery which was to come out in full force after Moore's first visit to Greece, in 1951.

Altogether, then, Moore in the middle years of the war was thrashing around like some powerful mechanism that had somehow got disconnected from its proper function: like a locomotive in a ploughed field, one might say. In 1943 this was put partly to rights when he was commissioned to carve a 'Madonna and Child' for St Matthew's Church, Northampton. Fifty-nine inches high, and in his favourite Hornton stone, this was to occupy him for the best part of a year. Once again, premonitory drawings can be found (dated 1942); but it is clear from the twelve small maquettes which have survived that in the preliminary stages

Moore was, as it were, negotiating between his own previous practice and his recollections of Florentine sculpture. A Florentine sweetness and tenderness are uppermost in the final work, but it would be a mistake to underestimate the element of toughness in what is probably the most immediately and universally attractive of all Moore's sculptures.

One early maquette keeps close to the Sainsbury *Mother and Child* of 1931. Another looks forward to the crowned Madonna which Moore was to realize for Claydon, in Suffolk, several years later. A third harks back to the profiled, relief-like sculptures of the late 1920s. A fourth, to the elongated frontal figures of 1931–2. Two others incorporate the wartime wall in the form of a summary throne. (The throne idea was, for that matter, already sketched out in a seated figure of 1928.) From the pre-war reclining figures Moore lifted an idea of drapery that served to mark off the area between the legs and give even the most naturalistic figure a formal interest, below the knee, that matched the charm and eloquence of the contrasted

2 Figures in a setting *Pen, chalk and watercolour*
3 in. × 22 in. 1942 *Artist's Collection*

93 Figures in a setting *Gouache and watercolour*
18 in. × 22 in. 1942 Joseph Pulitzer Jun., St Louis

heads. For the heads themselves, a whole gamut of formulae was tried out, from the pin-pierced hominoid forms of the pre-war reclining figures to the mask-forms of 1928–9 and, in the final maquette, something not far from a naturalistic English-rose ideal of the Madonna. In all this, Moore was faced with one of the cardinal difficulties of the figure-subject in twentieth-century painting and sculpture. Ever since Gauguin, that is to say, eloquence in the figure-subject has been a matter not of circumstantial detail but of the purity and intensity of the emotional gesture which is involved. In a painting like Gauguin's *Te Rerioa – The Dream* in the Courtauld Galleries there is an incongruity between the treatment of the girls' faces, which approximates to orthodox portrait-style, and the treatment of the rest of their bodies, which aims at an entirely different kind of eloquence; and this incongruity jars more and more, as we become more and more accustomed to kinds of painting in which old-style 'accuracy' plays no part. It is partly for this reason that paintings like Picasso's *Ambroise Vollard* of 1910 now seem

to us much more 'like' than portraits by Mancini or Orpen: the imaginative thrust is what counts. Moore in general has allowed the body to define the character of his figures, when character enters into them at all. Where ever other part, it is mistaken policy to give one par the head, references of a sort which are denie to the others and are in any case irrelevant t the kind of work of art which the artist is aimin at. But in this instance, and in that of th Claydon *Madonna and Child*, Moore risks naturalistic approach.

There were two main difficulties in this. On is that every naturalistic idiom dates: the othe that there might be an unmeaningful jump o style between the face of the Madonna and th rest of the piece. In the Northampton Madonna both difficulties were averted. Neither face ha dated: and Moore contrived to carry over from the faces to the rest of the sculpture, and bac again, the same slow, grand, unaccente rhythms. Detail-photographs bring this out ver well, for if we look at them as notations of form and without trying to identify the passage i

Sculpture in landscape *Pen and watercolour* 1940
'right S. Ludington, Santa Barbara, California

96 Crowd looking at a tied-up object *Pen, chalk wash
and watercolour 17 in. × 22 in. 1942 Sir Kenneth Clark*

Girl reading to a woman holding a child *Pen,
alk and watercolour* 1942 *Private Collection*

97 Drawing *Pen and wash* 1942 *Private Collection*

98 Madonna and Child *Hornton stone 59 in.* 1943-4
Church of St Matthew, Northampton

question in the general context of the piece, we shall find that a kindred swell and flow characterize every one of its areas: brow rhymes with shoulder, cheek with knee, chin with elbow, neck with ankle. So compelling is the basic rhythm of the piece that even where incongruities occur they pass unnoticed. How many people notice, or care, that the feet of the Madonna are the feet of the Leeds *Reclining Figure* of 1929, or that the draperies are a filled-in version of some of the Stringed Figures of 1937–8? What matters is that the feet have just that minimum of characterization which prevents the sculpture from coming to a full stop at its base; similarly the horizontal, deeply indented line of the draperies offsets the vertical line of the forelegs and prevents the sculpture from being, at that point, all leg.

To the layman, the astonishing thing at the time was that an *avant-garde* sculptor like Moore could produce something with such immediate human appeal. To those who had followed his career, however, the astonishing thing was that he should have employed within the naturalistic idiom of the piece as a whole so many of the formal devices which he had developed in sculptures generally held to be entirely hermetic. The 'lifelike' modelling of the hands and the inimitably 'suitable' neckline of the Madonna's dress were not what some people took them to be: gestures of reassurance on the part of a reformed revolutionary. Their function is to keep the observer busy and interested at crucial points in the general design. Imagine those hands as flat pads of unworked stone, or that area between neck and breast as perfectly smooth, and you will see that something altogether more rude would have resulted. The point of the Northampton *Madonna and Child* is that the observer shifts back and forth, unwittingly, between the idiom of Easter Island and the idiom of George Eliot, and that the two are made to blend without incongruity. We end up by not quite knowing whether what we are looking at is an abstract composition in three perfectly-judged dimensions or a straight portrait of a well-built young Yorkshire mother with a commendably sober taste in embroidery.

99 Sketch for Dartington memorial figure *Bronze 7 in.*
1945 *Artist's Collection*

(One would say of her, as George Eliot says of Dorothea Brooke in *Middlemarch*, that she has 'that kind of beauty which seems to be thrown into relief by poor dress'.)

It was an achievement not easy to repeat, even if Moore's inclinations had been towards repetition. But he did make several attempts in 1944 at family groups – father, mother, and either one or two children – and these eventually served for the Stevenage *Family Group* of 1948–9. When compared, however, with the elaborate terraced construction of the Northampton group these early sketches for a family group tend to look forlorn and stilted: the nobility of the initial gesture is not quite carried through, and the individual figures in each group remain undeniably apart. The undifferentiated bare surfaces of their bodies cause the eye to slide this way and that, nowhere finding either the fastidious detail of the Northampton group or the unifying rhythm which gives that group its tranquil majesty. And when he came, in 1947, to make a 'Family Group' on a slightly larger scale (sixteen inches high) he produced one (pl. 105) that combined a rather more naturalistic treatment of the parents' torsos with an altogether new invention, by which the two children were turned into a single basket-like form. Once again, a simultaneous approach from both extremes of the sculptor's idiom turned out to be imaginatively right.

Only once did Moore return to the untroubled majesty of the Northampton Madonna. This was the *Memorial Figure* (pl. 100) which he completed in 1945–6 in memory of Christopher Martin. Once or twice – in the feet, for instance, and in the emblematic treatment of the right ear – this looks back to the 'progressive' idiom of the 1930s, and of course the upraised right knee is a survival from an even earlier idiom: that of the Leeds *Reclining Figure* of 1929. What Moore would not have aimed at, at any earlier time, is the gentle flowing movement of the whole piece and the dialogue between the simplified draperies and the monumental forms beneath. Once again the head and the hands are just sufficiently characterized to quicken our interest just when the piece might have

100 Memorial Figure *Hornton stone 56 in.* 1945–6
Dartington Hall, Devon

egun to seem too uniformly general in tone: a
in-pricked turret and a pair of incised pads
would not have served. (A seven-inch terracotta
modello for the *Memorial Figure* makes relatively
little effect in these and other respects: Moore
had reached a stage in his career at which he
could pick out, one by one, the points at which
a piece needed to be simplified and accentuated.)

The *Memorial Figure* brings to an appro-
priately elegiac close the series of swathed
human figures, drawn or carved, which derive
in part from the experience of the shelter and in
part from the investigation of pure sculptural
form. Like the Northampton Madonna, it presents the experience of the shelter in sublimated
state; as for the investigation of form, it is carried on discreetly and in such a way as to
frighten no one. One might also infer, and some
people did infer, that Moore by 1945 was like
Prospero in Act V, scene 1: a once-terrifying
figure who had abjured his rough magic. In no
two pieces, certainly, is Moore's tender side so
much in evidence. But Moore would cease to
exist, as an artist, if either 'the tough' or 'the

tender' were to get the upper hand for long
and it was only a matter of time (and of trans-
port, at the end of the war) before he could say,
with Prospero:

> the strong based promontory
> Have I made shake and by the spurs pluck'd up
> The pine and cedar: graves at my command
> Have waked their sleepers, oped, and let 'em forth
> By my so potent art.

V 1945-1954

was in 1945, after the end of the war in
urope, that Henry Moore took up the position
hich he has held ever since: that of the
nglishman who comes top of the list when
ving art is in question. Older people then, and
ounger people now, could command private
yalties no less intense; but Moore's particular
osition springs from the fact that in life, as in
rt, he can move easily and unaffectedly from
e private to the public role (and back again).
e is a natural ambassador. At home in all
ocieties, he has kept something within him of
e young man from Yorkshire who thought
at nothing in the world could be more won-
erful than riding on top of a London bus; and
is sense of wonder and fun communicates
self whenever he undertakes what, to other
rtists, might seem a ceremonious chore.

By the end of 1945, therefore, he was a
rustee of the Tate Gallery, a member of the
rts Council's Art Panel, and an Honorary
octor of Literature in the University of Leeds:
ese were prototypes of the honours which were
come to him more profusely than to any
nglish artist since the days of Leighton and
oynter. When he went back to Paris, in
ovember 1945, it was almost as an official

visitor; and whereas twenty years earlier he had
turned away in timidity from Maillol's door,
Brancusi himself now bothered to come in from
the Impasse Ronsin to see him. In 1946 he paid
his first visit to New York, where the Museum
of Modern Art gave him a major retrospective
exhibition, and in 1948 he made the decisive
breakthrough to international status when he
was awarded the Grand Prize for Sculpture at
the Twenty-fourth Venice Biennale. From this
point onwards he was an accepted public figure,
with all the acclaim, and much also of the con-
secrated boredom, which that phrase implies.
Not to have called on Henry Moore came to be
the equivalent of 'miss three turns' in snakes
and ladders for foreign collectors, museum
directors, and miscellaneous enthusiasts when
they visited England. Not to have Moore on a
committee meant, in official art circles, the loss
of a leaven of good nature and good sense. And
Moore's journeys abroad took on, in spite of
himself, the character of an official progress, in
which every remark was noted down by the
local Eckermann and every invitation had overtones of Old Diplomacy.

All this meant a radical change, not in
Moore himself, but in his relations with the

102 Reclining Figure *Elmwood 75 in.* 1945–6 *Cranbrook
Academy of Art, Michigan*

outer world. If we rule out the interval of war, it was only six working-years since a historian of English sculpture had felt it necessary to say that Moore should not be confused with Henry Moore, R.A., an eminent Victorian amply represented in Sir Henry Tate's initial gift to his eponymous Gallery. Nor had he moved far, in financial terms, from the days in which five pounds had to see him through for a week's sojourn in Paris: fifty shillings for a return fare by night boat from Newhaven to Dieppe, and fifty shillings for board and lodging and incidental expenses in Paris itself. Doubtless it was pleasant to be acknowledged, but the Parkhill Road group had never lacked confidence, any more than they had worried about money. By 1930 Moore had, after all, been on terms of personal acquaintance with the nine or ten people who counted in the world of *avant-garde* sculpture. In 1929, for instance, the Leeds *Reclining Figure* had been sent to an international exhibition of sculpture in Zürich, where it was shown with work by Lipchitz and others. Lipchitz had singled out the piece at once,

and when the two met in Paris in 1930 he was outstandingly generous about it and about Moore's potentialities as an international figure.

The world of sculpture was very small [Moore said recently], and even as a young man from England you could get to know all the people who counted. I knew Lipchitz and Zadkine and Giacometti by 1933, and Arp from about 1933 onwards, and I was really rather glad not to have an English 'tradition of sculpture' behind me. Paris was never really sculpture-minded, of course, and there was no such thing as an Ecole de Paris in sculpture as there was in painting. There were just a few individuals, whom one got to know. And the French critics didn't know the British Museum, or the Musée de l'Homme, let alone the whole history of sculpture, so they didn't realize what was happening when Gonzalea, for instance, got hold of the statue of the war-god Gou from Dahomey in the Musée de l'Homme. But I'd known since 1921, from what I'd seen in the British Museum, that the whole repertory of form-ideas was there, waiting to be picked up. Picasso and the British Museum were the only sources that I ever really needed.

103 Family Group *Bronze 60 in.* 1948–9 *Tate Gallery, London; Museum of Modern Art, New York*

With Picasso Moore has never had more than minimal direct contact, and of course there comes a time in the life of every major artist when he no longer needs the kind of stimulation which can be given by such contacts in his twenties and thirties. Moore remembers very well, however, an occasion in 1937 when he and Mrs Moore were in Paris and they happened to go and call on Picasso.

It was at the time of the Spanish War. A whole party of us had hoped to go to Spain – Auden and Spender and Blackett and Bernal and people like that – and Alexander Calder wanted to go along too, but at the last moment we weren't allowed to. Anyway, there we were in Paris, and there was a big lunch with Giacometti, Max Ernst, Paul Eluard, André Breton, and Irina and me, and it was all tremendously lively and I think that even Picasso was excited by the idea of our going to his studio. But when we got there he lightened the mood of the whole thing, as he loved to do. *Guernica* was still a long way from being finished. It was like a cartoon just laid in in black and grey, and he could have coloured it as he coloured the

sketches. You know the woman who comes running out of the cabin on the right with one hand held in front of her? Well, Picasso told us that there was something missing there, and he went and fetched a roll of paper and stuck it in the woman's hand, as much as to say that she'd been caught in the bathroom when the bombs came. That was just like him – to be so tremendously moved about Spain and yet turn it aside as a joke.

That had been in 1937: and now, only a year or two later (in working terms), Moore was an international figure. Not everyone survives a change of this sort, but Moore has used money and fame primarily as a way of cutting down on wasted effort and time. He still has the house near Much Hadham which he took in October 1940, after his studio in London had been bombed: it is a little bigger now, and a shade more comfortable, but fundamentally his way of life is what it always was. Nor did his habits of work change with success, though some of his friends regretted, then as now, the time that he gave and still gives to public duties. In the context of those duties it is worth recalling Moore's

104 King and Queen *Bronze 64½ in.* 1952–3 *W. J. Keswick, Glenkiln, Scotland*

105 Family Group *Bronze 16½ in.* 1947 *National Gallery of Victoria, Melbourne*

description of his working day in the early 1930s, when he had a cottage near Canterbury and Bernard Meadows was his assistant.

We'd all get up at 5.30 and throw a bucket of water over each other to make sure that we were thoroughly awake, and then we'd go on with whatever work we'd been doing the day before. Irina got our breakfast at 6.30 and by 7 o'clock we'd be at work in the open – I had five acres of shelving ground that ran down into a valley with hills on the other side. Any bit of stone stuck down in that field looked marvellous – like a bit of Stonehenge, but not so big. About 11.30 we'd get into our little Standard coupé and go down to the sea and bathe and eat our sandwiches, be back by 1.30 or 2, go on working till tea at 5 and then on again till dark. It made a 14-hour day, right through the summer, but it was like a holiday, compared with London.

The sea is a long way from Much Hadham, and I wouldn't put money on the continuance of the bucket-of-water reveille, but basically this is the kind of life that produced, within a year of the armistice in western Europe, both the *Memorial Figure* which has just been dis-

cussed and the even larger *Reclining Figure* i elmwood which was bought by the Cranbroo Academy of Art in Bloomfield Hills, Michiga The Cranbrook Academy figure is one of th high points of Moore's *œuvre*. It was forecast i detail in a drawing of 1942, and when Moor came to carve it there was very little to be e perimented with in the terracotta maquette The case for adumbrated breasts could be s against the case for the kind of pectoral she which was used in the huge reliefs of 1959, b beyond that the idea-structure was already i existence and could be drawn complete on th flat side of the block.

There is a basic difference, as I see it, b tween post-war figures such as this one and th Reclining Figures of the 1930s. Moore ha learnt from the experience of carving th Northampton *Madonna and Child* that if the bas rhythms were broad and firm enough th sculpture could combine the thrust of pu three-dimensional idea with direct naturalist reference. In the 1930s one or the other was pr dominant: if the idea was uppermost, as in th

106 Family Group *Bronze 17½ in. 1946 Phillips Gallery, Washington*

07 Three Standing Figures *Darley Dale stone 7 ft.*
947–8 *Battersea Park, London*

108 Five Figures (interiors for lead helmets) *Lead*
5 in. 1950 Artist's Collection

109 Reclining Figure *Hornton stone 30 in.* 1949
R. Sturgis Ingersoll, Philadelphia

o The Helmet *Lead 12 in.* 1940 *Roland Penrose*

111 Maquette for openwork head no. 1 *Bronze 7 in.*
1950 *Kurt Valentin Gallery Inc., New York*

2 Helmet Head no. 2 *Bronze 14 in.* 1950 *Private collection*

113 Upright External Internal Form *Bronze 6 ft. 7 in.*
1952–3 *Artist's Collection*

Corsehill stone *Reclining Figure* (pl. 44) of 1934–5,
then the human references were inscrutable. If
truth to everyday experience came first, as in
the Sainsbury *Mother and Child* of 1932, then the
sculptural idea took second place : the Sainsbury
piece could be an illustration to Chateaubriand's
Atala with no more than superficial adjustment.
But in the Cranbrook Academy figure the two
things exist side by side : or, more exactly, end
to end, for whereas the legs and feet are related
to those of the Onslow-Ford figure of 1939 the
torso is based, as Sir Kenneth Clark was the
first to point out, on one of the classic themes of
Western sculpture. After twenty and more years
of determinedly not using the 'Greek spectacles'
to which academic sculpture had been subject,
Moore suddenly slipped them back on again in
order to adapt to his own purposes a theme
mooted in the Parthenon frieze and thereafter
constantly recurrent in Western art : the figure,
as Sir Kenneth put it, 'with averted thorax and
open legs, struggling out of the earth like a tree,
not without a powerful suggestion of sexual
readiness'. The relevant passage in *The Nude*
also speaks of 'the pulsation of the wooden
heart, like a crusader's head, burrowing in the
hollow breast', and goes on to take the Cranbrook Academy figure as an instance of the way
in which in modern art 'the nude does not
simply represent the body, but relates it, by
analogy, to all other structures that have become part of our imaginative experience'. And
the particular point, here, is that in the 1930
Moore's sculptures either did or did not appear
unequivocally to universal conscious experience.
In this piece, Moore jumps from one position
to the other with no sense of strain, and we
move without incongruity from the very
beautiful nuzzling form, which could stand for
lover, son, heart, or child unborn, to the turret-
like head and the cavernous leg-forms of Moore's
practice in the 1930s.

This was, even so, an isolated occasion. In
Moore's other work during the immediate post-
war era there is an eddying back and forth
between experimental, opened-out, and naturalistic, neo-Classical draped figures. In the small
bronze *Reclining Figure* of 1945 the human
figure is seen as a steep-pitched catchment-area,
but in some of the small family groups there are
echoes of the Promised-Land atmosphere which
descended on England as the war came to an

15 Helmet Head and Shoulders *Bronze 6½ in.* 1952
Private Collection

16 Head and Shoulders *Bronze 17½ in.* 1950 *Dr
an der Wal, Amsterdam*

nd. An idealized wholesomeness comes over
ne notion of the family, which Moore knows as
vell as anyone to be fraught, in reality, with
otential tension and stress. This was one of the
noments in history when people believed that
 was possible to make a new start in human
ffairs. And where better to make that new
 art than with the family?

The New Town was, in this context, the pre-
estined setting for the New Family, and in
948 Moore was commissioned to make a large
roup of mother, father, and child for Barclay
chool in Stevenage. There was about the com-
nission, if not about the finished group, some-
ning of the generalized uplift of electioneering.
Moore is a man with a highly developed sense
f social duty, but I myself find the *Family
roup* less successful than the Northampton
Madonna and Child in negotiating the dangerous
round between simplicity and flatness. More
recisely, I feel that so large and elaborate a
iece needs a little more of the tough side of
Moore's nature. The Northampton Madonna is
nder to the point of sweetness; but this quality
 offset by an implied ferocity in the radical
eatment of the lower limbs. (Some years after
ne family group commissions had been com-
leted, Moore returned to the theme of the two
ated figures in the *King and Queen* of 1952.)

Moore's basic gift, as it seems to me, is more
r the telling analogy and the multiple refer-
nce than for the identifiable human situation.
 significant piece, in this context, is the *Three
tanding Figures* (pl. 107) of 1947–8, which is now
 Battersea Park. In many ways this derives
om the imaginary figure groups of the war-
me drawings; but it also relates to the idea of
ne watcher or witness which, pioneered by
V. H. Auden in the 1930s, came up strongly in
ne work of Reg Butler and Lynn Chadwick
 the 1950s. The man or woman who watches
ne skies has a particular emotional meaning
r anyone who, from the Spanish Civil War
nwards, has looked on the skies primarily as a
otential source of catastrophe, and in carving
nis group Moore drew, whether consciously or
ot, on the stored memories of millions. This
ives the group a distinct historical importance,
ut it does not of itself make it a major work of
rt. Judged purely as a three-dimensional
nvention the *Three Standing Figures* do not
em to me to rank very high among Moore's

achievements. The swathed cylindrical figures
have, in fact, something of that 'decorative and
linear stylization' which Moore once pointed
to in the post-Gudean period of Sumerian art.

Altogether this was a difficult period for
Moore. On the one hand he needed to go on
consolidating the private fancies which had
welled up since 1939 and had had no chance of
three-dimensional expression. On the other,
people were looking to him for public utterances
of the kind which had been forced upon him by
history. He was getting the kind of acclaim and
consecration which is usually accorded to
Grand Old Men in their eighties: and official
approval of this sort is designed as much to
smother further progress as to favour a realistic
appraisal of what has been done hitherto. New
experiences were coming to him, nevertheless,
on every hand. In 1946, for instance, his
daughter was born: and the image of the family
took on a new, leaping, unpredictable intensity.
A journey to Greece in 1951 had almost as great
an impact as the first journey to Italy, just
twenty-five years earlier. Professionally speaking, the context of his work changed considerably with the arrival in the early 1950s of what
came to be called 'the younger British sculptors'.
Moore took on, in relation to them, the status
of a senior master. The use of welded iron by
Butler, Chadwick, and Adams emphasized the
basic fullness and roundness of Moore's forms,
just as the entry of a trumpet at the top of the
orchestra will make the first 'cello sound deeper
and richer. Everything in art was on the move.

In the circumstances it would have been in-
human if Moore had not manifested some
variant of uncertainty at this time. (One sheet
of drawings, dated 1948, is a kind of chart of
alternatives, including as it does a naturalistic
female nude and a naturalistic horse, side by
side with preliminary sketches for the Internal
and External Forms and the Helmet Heads of a
year or two later.) Meanwhile, the Claydon
Madonna and Child in Hornton stone was carved
in 1948–9 after a small maquette of 1943; and
as late as 1954–5 the Harlow *Family Group* was
carved from a maquette of 1944. These were
major works, in point of size, but in style they
looked back and not forward. Somewhere
within the Claydon group is the idea of internal
and external form, but that idea is muffled in
naturalistic detail and there is a certain clash of

117 Helmet Head no. 1 *Bronze* 13½ *in.* 1950 *Private Collection*

118 Animal Head *Bronze 12 in.* 1951 *Peter Pears Collection*

style between the Florentine graces of the Madonna's head and crown and the almost Mexican heaviness of her draped legs and very large feet. The Harlow group could be catalogued under the heading of 'Civic virtues, apotheosis of'; and although there are beautiful passages of naturalistic modelling here and there the general tone is rather sententious and the length of towelling which loops in and out of the parents' legs is not a device which would have satisfied Moore at any other time in his career.

Unluckily, we should have to go to the U.S.A. to see the piece which proves that Moore the all-risking poet was still very much alive. This is the Hornton stone *Reclining Figure* (pl. 109) of 1949. After many Reclining Figures in which a central hole was the dominant compositional feature here is one in which, on the contrary, the central area is filled in. Such is the modelling of that area that two complementary movements are set up: one begins below the heart and swings up and away to the left, while the other begins at the bottom of the right thigh

and swings up and away to the right. The relationship, here, between the thing seen and the thing imagined is one of the most moving in all Moore's work, in that the spreading and subtly modulated area between heart and knees is continuously alive in terms both of human anatomy and of the landscape-analogy, the sublimations of moorland and bluff, which Moore keeps going at the same time. This is not one of Moore's largest carvings – it is only thirty inches long – but it is one in which social duty is laid aside and the imagination runs free to glorious effect.

Among the ideas mooted just before the outbreak of war and not yet allowed their full expression was one which appears in a water-colour-and-chalk drawing of 1939 and was worked up in three small sculptures a few months later. Moore had conceived of a small sculpture which would be both head and helmet, armour and living organism, internal and external form. Thus described, it might seem to have timely martial associations, but in point of fact the implications of the Helmet pieces are a

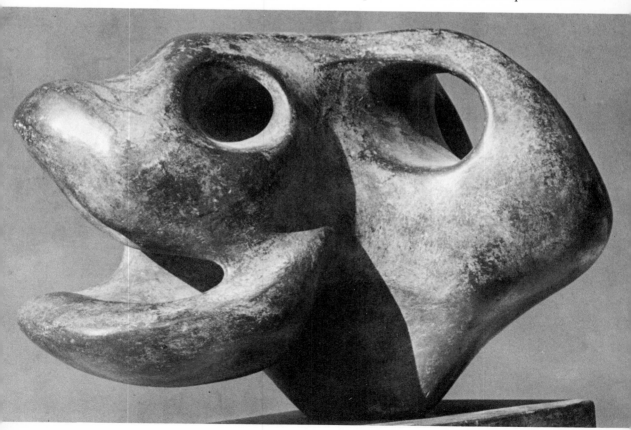

118

good deal more complex. It is uncertain, for instance, whether the internal figure is protected or imprisoned by the helmet itself: whether it has, in short, got into a situation which it can no longer control. From the way in which this idea went on battering for Moore's attention until well into the 1960s we can assume that it has a particular significance for him. It has to do, above all, with envelopment. Within the fulfilled and rounded form is its antithesis: a form that is angular, irregular, uneasy, often forked and frantic. Nature herself set the tone by making the skull one of the most regular and predictable of known objects, and the skull's contents so absolutely erratic and mysterious. Moore from the first gave his outer coverings the grand flawless outline of a Greek helmet: what sits within is various enough for the findings of psychiatry. Sometimes it suggests a Cycladic figure, sometimes a shoe-tree. Sometimes it relates to prehistory, sometimes to an uncatalogued form of microphone. Once inside the outer covering it can never be seen completely: when not inside, it looks incomplete and defenceless. The combined figures are, in short, nearer to mother and child, or to mother and foetus, than to any manual of warfare.

These remarks do not apply, however, to the openwork heads which were also produced in 1950. In these, helmet and head are undeniably one: and their oneness is the whole subject of the sculpture. (Moore's illustrations for Goethe's *Prometheus*, which appeared in 1950, have a lot in common with these openwork heads.) In 1951 Moore was inspired to push the helmet-and-head idea still further: a drawing of that year develops the notion, which in other hands would have had a directly erotic content, of an armoured female nude, in which it is hard to tell where the breastplate ends and the naked human breast takes over. The resulting bronze *Helmet Head and Shoulders* was produced a year later and is one of the most purely elegant of Moore's small pieces.

The idea of the internal and external form was transferred, meanwhile, to an altogether grander and more ambitious context. As early as 1931 Moore had aimed, in the green Hornton stone *Composition* (pl. 32), to 'get one form to stay alive inside another': and from 1951 he took the idea of the form half-protected, half-imprisoned by another form and developed it on

121 Working Model for Reclining Figure (Internal and External Forms) *Bronze length 21 in. 1951 Private Collection*

123 Reclining Figure *Bronze length 7 ft. 6 in. 1951 Arts Council, London*

122 Reclining Figure (External Form) *Bronze length 7 ft. 1952–3 Museum of Modern Art, Rome*

the scale, and with many of the implications, of a full-length standing figure. Once again the most imposing of these sculptures, the 103-inch-high elmwood carving *Internal and External Forms* of 1953–4, is in the U.S.A. (at the Albright Art Gallery, Buffalo): and its dimensions are such that it is unlikely to revisit this country. But the theme is one that Moore used for a number of smaller pieces that were cast in bronze: as late as 1965 an edition of the *Upright Interior Form* (*Flower*), of 1951 was produced, and in general the idea obviously means a great deal to him. To the late Erich Neumann, whose *Henry Moore und der Archetyp des Weiblichen* Moore speaks of with friendly wariness and has steadfastly refused to read, the internal-and-external form was the culmination of all his work to date.

What we see here [he wrote of the Albright piece], is the mother bearing the still-unborn child within her and holding the born child again in her embrace. But this child is the dweller within the body, the psyche itself, for which the body, like the world, is merely the circumambient space that shelters or casts out. It is no accident that this

figure reminds us of those Egyptian sarcophagi in the form of mummies, showing the mother goddess as the sheltering womb that holds and contains the dead man like a child again, as at the beginning. Mother of life, mother of death, and all-embracing body-self, the archetypal mother of man's germinal ego consciousness – this truly great sculpture of Moore's is all these in one.

It is rude to contradict, and Moore's German admirers have had a rough ride in England ever since one of them asserted that, as an Englishman, Moore was doubtless more familiar with Ossian than with Homer. Without disputing that the piece in question will bear Neumann's interpretation, we are entitled to remark that it is also rather like a hollow tree, that many such trees can be found on the borders of Moore's property in Hertfordshire, and that the lignum vitae *Composition* of 1933 (pl. 145) is not far, in terms of sculptural idea, from the Albright piece. It is possible, in short, that Moore did not have anything like so portentous an ambition when he made the piece, and that it represents primarily a new and up-ended formal solution

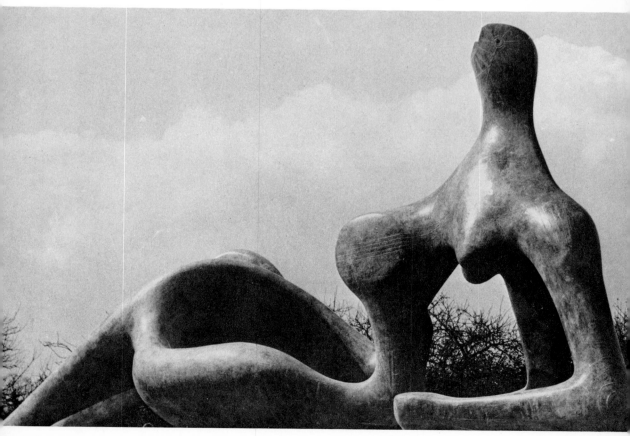

124 AUGUSTE RODIN Torso of a Young Woman
Bronze 33¼ in. 1909

25 Draped Torso *Bronze 35 in. 1953 Ferens Art Gallery, Hull*

126 Draped Torso *Bronze 35 in.* 1953 *Ferens Art Gallery,*
Hull

27 Fallen Warrior (first stage) *Plaster length 50 in.*
956 *Artist's Collection*

f a problem that he had often tackled in Reclining Figures. Laid flat, the huge piece would look like an early draft for part of the great *Reclining Mother and Child* of 1960–1. Erect, looks a little like an opened-out version of one f the cowled figures of the early 1930s. The nternal form, with its bird-head and wasted ether limbs, certainly looks as if it needed projection, but the smoothness and benignity of the xternal form do not, in that case, look quite ough enough. For a landmark in Moore's *œuvre* should, in fact, point rather to the small twenty-one inches) working model (pl. 121) for reclining figure which is also dated 1951. In his, the alliance of inner and outer forms seems o me altogether more cogent, and the upward hrust of the inquisitive turret-head is an inired return to the idiom of the St Louis *eclining Figure* (pl. 46) of 1933. The outer form visibly an *active* envelopment of the inner one: nd the relationship between outer and inner orms is one of like with like and not, as in the lbright figure, one of antitheses. Moore is rongest, as I see it, when the internal-and-

external theme relates to contrast between equal partners; and although I have no warrant for saying that he agrees, it is on record that when he planned a vulnerable, tuber-like form to go inside the *Reclining Figure (External Form)* of 1952–3 (pl. 122) he eventually gave up the idea and published the external form as a piece on its own. This may have been partly because the vacant inner spaces set up some of the grandest echoes in all Moore: but it was also, I suspect, because there was something basically abhorrent to him in the invalidish forms of the projected internal piece.

I have run on ahead, meanwhile, of another cardinal piece in Moore's development: the *Reclining Figure* which was first shown at the Festival of Britain in 1951. This is more than life-size (ninety inches long) and it is Moore's most ambitious shot at making the spaces between the forms as important, and as various, as the forms themselves. It is, in fact, a parallel in Moore-terms to the welded iron figure or quasi-figure which was pioneered by Gonzalez, taken up by Butler in the early 1950s, and

128 and 129 Fallen Warrior (first stage) *Plaster*
length 50 in. 1956 *Artist's Collection*

arried forward by Chillida ten years later. The ronze itself is used for a kind of drawing-in-he-air: the areas which it defines and leaves acant are at least as much the subject of the culpture as are the areas which it defines and lls in. The turret and the upraised knees remain from the 1930s, but the vacancies give the iece a monumentality which is not earth-ound: Moore here commands the air. For the rst time in his career, he had produced a piece f which no one drawing could give anything ke the total effect: for there was no longer any principal view' or 'best view' from which that otal effect could be summarized.

And the piece is one from which many later nspirations derived. Draped, it became the ime-Life figure of 1952–3. The *King and Queen* f 1952–3, the *Sculptural Object* of 1960, and even ne *Two-piece Reclining Figure* of 1961 – all can e traced eventually and in part to the 1951 igure. One final point: Moore offset the bone-mooth surface of the bronze with a network of ne raised lines that in some places run counter o the movement of the form and in other places emphasize it; and this, also marks a watershed in his *œuvre* in that in almost all later pieces he goes for what he once called 'the elephant look' of bronze: the look half-way between leather and meat. The 1951 piece has, on the contrary, a fine-drawn calligraphical quality.

The year 1951 was also the occasion of Moore's first visit to Greece. This was occasioned by the arrival in Athens of the British Council's touring exhibition of his work, and it took him not only to Athens but to Mycenae, Corinth, Delphi, and elsewhere. Moore by that time was of course a very different human being and a vastly more evolved artist than the young man who had gone to Italy just twenty-five years earlier. There was no question, therefore, of a commotion comparable to that which marked the year 1926. There was no question, either, of his finding in Greek art, whether Classical or pre-Classical, the kind of general authorization which he had found elsewhere. His is, as I have indicated, a northerly and a burrowing, under-ground *inside* orientation, for all the pleasure that he takes in seeing his work out of doors.

132 AUGUSTE RODIN Study of a Seated Woman (Cybele) *Bronze 19¾ in. c. 1889 Mr and Mrs Max Wasserman, Chesnut Hill, Massachusetts*

133 Draped Reclining Figure *Plaster for Bronze length 62 in. 1952–3 Time-Life Building, London*

His caves are northern caves and his promontories nearer to Flamborough Head than to the Argive coast.

Greece is Greece, and it would be a dull and trivial nature that did not respond to it. But when, two years later, Moore produced the *Draped Torso* (pls. 125, 126) that could loosely be called Greekish we were reminded as much of Rodin's *Torso of a Young Woman* of 1909 (pl. 124) as of any particular Greek model. And the *Warrior with Shield* of 1953–4 (pl. 131) is, again, closer to Rodin's little *Study of a Seated Woman* (*Cybele*) of *c.* 1889 (pl. 132) than to any martial figure that Moore had seen in Greece. What are usually called Moore's Greekish figures do, in fact, seem to me to have a distinct air of the turn of the century about them. They are, too, among the earliest of the pieces in which his loyalty is given over entirely to bronze : and not only to bronze in general but to the quintessence of the material. I myself miss the multifarious interest of Moore's materials in the 1920s and 1930s (when Braque, for instance, came to Moore's studio just after the war, he was particularly taken with the speckled, grainy, subtly coloured aspect of the cast concrete *Mask* (pl. 26) of 1929, but there is no gainsaying the powerful role which bronze itself plays in the work of the 1950s and 1960s. And nothing could be less Greek than the broody, not to say sullen look of the material, with its hint of enormous burdens and romantic defiances.

The argument for Greece rests, in fact, on two things. One is the use of drapery in pieces like the Time-Life figure of 1952-3. The other is the choice of subjects vaguely related to those of Greek art, like the *Warrior with Shield* and the brutalized *Falling Warrior* (pl. 136) of 1956-7. Moore himself dealt with the first when he wrote some notes on the Time-Life figure. The experience of the blanketed figures in the Shelter drawings had convinced him, he said, that he ought one day to experiment with the use of more naturalistic draperies: and 'my first visit to Greece in 1951 perhaps helped to strengthen this intention'.

Drapery [he went on] can emphasize the tension in a figure, for where the form pushes outwards, such as on the shoulders, the thighs, the breasts, etc., it can be pulled tight across the form (almost like a bandage), and by contrast with the crumpled slackness of the drapery which lies between the salient points, the pressure from inside is intensified. Also in my mind was to connect the contrast of the sizes of folds, here small, fine, and delicate, in other places big and heavy, with the form of mountains, which are the crinkled skin of the earth. (The analogy, I think, comes out in close-up photographs taken of the drapery alone.)

Moore has never written a loose or an irrelevant word, and this particular text disposes altogether, in my view, of the idea that the draped statues owe anything substantial to Greek art. A sculptor like Johann Gottfried Schadow (1764-1850) used neo-Classical drapery to make an effect which related to his own time, and not to that of the second century B.C.: and Moore, likewise, uses it to romantic ends that would have been incomprehensible to the Greeks. The 'crinkled skin of the earth' was not something that they would have thought of as a metaphor for the folds of costume, but it was one of the quintessential metaphors for emotional states in the England of the 1940s and 1950s. Look at John Piper or Geoffrey Grigson

on the derivations of British Romantic painting, and you will find, over and over again, topographical references of this sort: drapery, for Moore, was another way, and a new one, of mediating between landscape and the human body.

The reference in his text to photography is also important to our understanding of his work, for Moore is a gifted photographer whose work in the medium constitutes a kind of authorized non-verbal commentary on his sculptures. It cannot be an accident that his photographs reach their level of maximum eloquence at just the period when his sculptures are ever-more concerned with the specific character of bronze. Detail-photographs of the draped figures are, for that matter, one of the most rewarding of quasi-creative activities for anyone who can hold a camera at the appropriate range. There is almost no category of landscape, from glacier to moraine and from dry river-bed to precipitous scree, which cannot be counterfeited in this way. Nor are we talking of a shoddy 'dramatic' effect: the photograph looks right, no matter how we construe it, and the thing photographed retains its dignity.

Next to the Shelter drawings, the draped figures are among the most popular of all Moore's works. This is partly, I think, because people look to them for a certain generalized melancholy. The *Draped Torso* (pls. 125, 126) of 195 might, in point of fact, be that of an Olympic gold medallist after an unusually heavy work out. But a more common interpretation is in terms of picturesque decay: the human figure, worn away by time, stands for civilization itself, too feeble by now to do more than give an elegiac appearance to the facts of decline. Moore discourages this, and specifically says of the Time-Life figure that it is 'not in slack repose but, as it were, alerted'. Yet the sculpture, not the text, is what we are talking about in the end and to most observers the tone of the piece is given by the picturesque disarray of the draperies and – no other word will do – the elegiac beauty, suggestive of a great tradition gone sweet and soft, which they confer on the body as a whole. For Moore himself, on the other hand, one lesson of the Draped Figure was that the possibilities of bronze could be played up a great deal harder than they had been played hitherto. If we see the draped

135 AUGUSTE RODIN The Martyr *Bronze*
40–47 *Metropolitan Museum of Art, New York*

136 Falling Warrior *Bronze 58 in. 1956–7 Private Collection*

137 Time-Life Screen Maquette no. 1 *Bronze*
7 in. × 13 in. 1952 Private Collection

138 Time-Life Screen Maquette no. 2 *Bronze*
7 in. × 13 in. 1952 Private Collection

139 Time-Life Screen Maquette no. 3 *Bronze*
7 *in.* × *13 in.* 1952 *Private Collection*

141 Working Model for Time-Life Screen *Bronze*
39½ in. × *15 in.* 1952 *Private Collection*

140 Time-Life Screen Maquette no. 4 *Bronze*
7 *in.* × *13 in.* 1952 *Private Collection*

142 Time-Life Screen *Portland stone 26 ft. 6 in.* × *10 ft*
1952 *Time-Life Building, London*

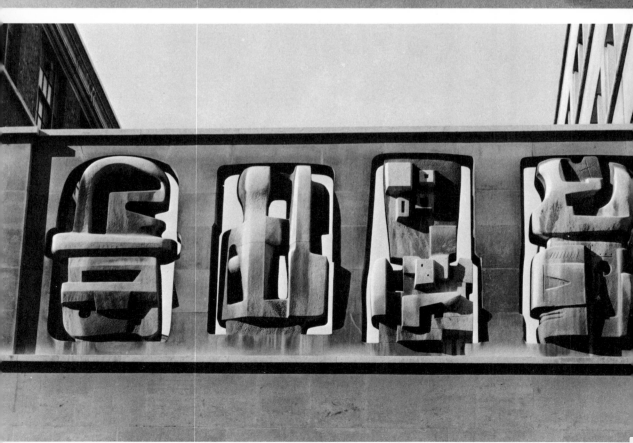

eces, in this sense, as midway between the
1oothness and roundness of the Internal-and-
xternal Figures and the calculated rugosities
the two- and three-piece Reclining Figures
the early 1960s we shall have got the point:
1d the point is that the big late bronzes are
lapted to a double perspective – that of the
an who comes upon them from a distance, as
might glimpse a great ruin from the air, and
at of the man who traverses them as a fly
ight traverse the Erectheum.
From the so-called (though not by Moore)
reek period there remain the two Warriors
1d their related maquettes. Dr Neumann
ought that the *Warrior with Shield* of 1953–4
as 'the most devastating portrayal in all art of
suprapersonal castration complex'. 'It shows',
: went on, 'complete capitulation before the
rces of destruction.' And although Neumann's
ook does not deal with the later *Falling Warrior*
ere is no doubt that these two do form a
yptic interlude in Moore's work, and one as to
hich no decisive explanation has yet come
rward. There is undeniably something odd
out the iconography of the two Warriors.
listaken as it may be to feel that every doughty
;hter must be a Hercules, it remains true that
oth Moore's warriors are conspicuously puny.
he *Falling Warrior* (pl. 136) adopts, moreover, a
ose that in another context might signify the
tremes of sexual fulfilment: and the fulfil-
ent, what is more, of a beautiful woman. This
ement of sexual ambiguity heightens the
rangeness which does not, in any case, have
1ything to do with Greece. Moore here seems
be close to Rodin – and to the Rodin who
id, 'The sculpture of antiquity sought the
gic of the human body. I seek its psychology.'
The Time-Life figure which I discussed above
as commissioned from Moore in combination
ith a sculptured screen which was to be visible
oth from the street and from the open court-
ard in which the reclining figure would be
aced. In the event, the project was hampered
/ the regulations which forbid the erection of
rge and heavy objects immediately above the
reet. For this reason Moore was not able to
rry out his original intention, which was that
ch of the four elements in the screen should
: able to move independently, thus making an
semble which would allow of regular varia-
on. Nor did the final version turn out altogether

happily, in that it had to be set so high above
the street, and the street at that point is so
narrow, that it is more or less invisible. Moore
has in fact said privately that he would give a
good deal to be able to take the screen away
and make use of the ideas which are prisoners
within it.

The progress of the project is, none the less,
an immensely interesting episode in Moore's
career, and the four maquettes in conjunction
with the working model and full-scale version
reveal a great deal about the movement of his
thought. He had encouraged us to investigate
the whole affair by publishing a characteristically undramatic account of the processes
involved.

The first of the four maquettes [pl. 137] I rejected
because I thought it too obvious and regular a
repetition of the fenestration of the building. In the
second maquette I tried to vary this and make it less
symmetrical, but in doing so the rhythms became
too vertical. In the third maquette I tried to
introduce a more horizontal rhythm but was
dissatisfied with the monotony of the size of the
forms. The fourth maquette [pl. 140] I thought was
better and more varied, and so this became the
definite maquette, although a further working
model produced other changes.

In point of fact, the maquettes represent a
run-through of nearly everything that Moore
had done before: a sounding-out of theme after
theme. Careful scrutiny will reveal standing
figures, reclining figures, animal heads, found
and altered objects, re-invented torsos, and
cryptic forms, half human being, half amphora,
half sea-worn pebble. The space in which these
are contained is the space of the pit-face drawings. The four final elements are pierced standing figures which have about them something
of relief and something of free-standing figure:
anatomy, in them, shades without warning into
the geometrical relief-forms of the 1930s. And
the screen looks forward, also, to many later
pieces: to the huge standing reliefs, for instance,
and to the pure sculptural inventions of the mid
1960s, to the Wall Reliefs of 1955, and to such
isolated pieces as the *Mother and Child: Hollow*
of 1959. Altogether, therefore, and even if the
commission did not work out as freely and
happily as had been hoped, the Time-Life
screen is a capital work in Moore's career.

VI 1955-1963

It was inevitable that one day, when the moment was right, the long series of Henry Moore's Reclining Figures would find its vertical counterpart. The vertical figure, in one or another of its manifestations, is vital to Moore, as it is vital also to the whole history of sculpture and, for that matter, to the English imagination. The English church-tower is one of the great products of our national imagination. Equally so, on a less exalted level, are the lighthouses and lookout-towers, so important to a sea-going and an island people. (I exclude, as being too obvious, the great repertory of upright figures and crosses which we share with the prehistory of all other ancient nations.)

To anyone as learned in the history of sculpture as is Henry Moore, the vertical figure is necessarily one of the great challenges. From the totems of the South Seas and the west coast of America down to the slender arrowy figures of Brancusi and Giacometti, much has been attempted. But much, even so, remains to be done, and we may be sure that Moore was storing ideas to this end for many years before he actually began work on the *Three Upright Motives* of 1955–6. Moore dates the initial impulse for these from the moment when he decided that a vertical figure, if anything, was needed to balance the horizontal lines of a new Olivetti building in Milan.

I visited the site [he wrote later], and a lone Lombardy poplar growing behind the building convinced me that a vertical work would act as the correct counterfoil to the horizontal rhythm of the building. . . . Back home in England I began the series of maquettes. I started by balancing different forms one above the other, with results rather like the North-West American totem-poles. But as I continued, the attempt gained more unity, and also perhaps more organic; and then one in particular [later to be named *Glenkiln Cross*] took on the shape of a crucifix: a kind of worn-down body and a cross merged into one.

'When I came', Moore went on, 'to carry out some of these maquettes in their final size, three of them grouped themselves together and, in my mind, assumed the aspect of a crucifixion scene, as though framed in the sky above Golgotha.' *In my mind*: these are three vital words, in the context, for Moore rarely discusses the 'meaning' of his work, and in this particular case what may seem to some an august identification may seem to others unnecessary and

144 Double Standing Figure *Bronze 7 ft. 3 in.* 1950
S. J. Salter, New York

limiting. (Moore went on to say: 'I do not especially expect others to find this symbolism in the group.')

The idea of standing figures grouped in threes dates, in any case, from several years earlier, and the idea of the standing figure itself from nearly thirty years before. Disregarding the naturalistic figures of the early 1930s, one could point to the African wood torso of 1927 (pl. 20) and a figure in beechwood from 1932 (pl. 36), in which the outline of the human body is reduced to a significant swelling, here and there, and a commanding knob of form at those points where Moore wished to hold our interest especially tight. They are still, in essence, naturalistic pieces: Nature's order, and Nature's hierarchy, are preserved: but their naturalism is one on to which a new idiom could be grafted. By 1938, when Moore produced the little *Stringed Figure* (pl. 67), which is less than six inches high, that grafting had been completed.

The stringed piece is, in fact, a key work in Moore's development. The 'head' has, to begin with, the horn- or handle-like characteristic which recurs in several major post-war pieces. In the threefold jutting which occurs between the 'neck' and the urn-like base there are foreshadowed the Upright Reliefs which are among the most enigmatic and disquieting of all Moore's works. In 1950, at a time when Authority hoped to have nothing but representational groups in perpetuity from a tamed and neo-conservative Moore, the *Double Standing Figure*, cast in bronze (pl. 144), announced a new, opened-out, linear approach to the figure, with flattened and triangular protrusions at shoulder height and slanted, rounded articulations at the waist. By comparison with the heavy-limbed human figures of a year or two before, these were animated wishbones, fleshless signals of a new idiom. In 1951 a drawing of three Standing Figures suggested that this idiom was getting beyond the schematic stage and might soon have a powerful emotional effect. Within a year a maquette, and within two years a group of three figures, twenty-eight inches high (pl. 155), proved this to be correct. All the spaces in the upper part of the body had now been filled in; and the stylization of heads and shoulders was considerably more abrupt, and more drastic, than in 1950. These forms had, in fact, a direct emotional impact which was stronger and more lasting than that of any of Moore's naturalistic heads. In the Northampton *Madonna and Child*, for instance, he had acquitted himself with honour in a task which, in the present state of sculpture, can be tackled by few artists of consequence. Individually and as a group the *Three Standing Motives* of 1953 derive from sources vastly more mysterious, and more personal to Moore, than the Madonnas and the Family Groups. They are recognizably human still, but drama of an inscrutable sort is in the air, and that drama resides as much in the attitudes struck by the figures as in the meta-morphoses which they have undergone.

Moore by now was at a stage in his career when it is more profitable to pursue his key themes in their sequence than to examine his output year by year. Now that practically the whole of his work was being cast in bronze he could work on five or six ideas simultaneously, and it is more rational to follow the evolution of these ideas in turn than to jump from one to another in terms of the date on which each appears to have been completed. In the 1950s, for instance, the Vertical Figure pushed its way into all kinds of enterprises, even if sometimes it had to be pushed out again – as happened, for instance, when Moore was invited to pre-pare the sculptural screen for an upper floor of the Time-Life building in London.

This commission had a particular interest for Moore, and for ourselves, in that he had always been, and for that matter is still, very much in two minds as to the possibilities of a happy relationship between sculptor and architect. In 1961 he said flatly, in conversation, that he had never wanted to work for architecture.

Either the sculpture is on the architecture, in which case it's only a one-sided object, or else it has a background of architecture, in which case the architect's vision is likely to dominate. It was different in the Renaissance, when a sculptor might be able to make his own architecture for his own sculpture. What I want is for the sculptor to have his own complete, self-contained existence. The idea that architecture is 'the mother of the arts' has put sculptors into the position of being the architects batmen. Architecture has never been the mother of the arts in that sense. All it has done is to house sculpture and painting: it gave the roof over the one, and provided a wall for the other, but the

149 Wall Relief no. 6 *Bronze 18½ in. × 13¼ in.* 1955
Marlborough Fine Art, London

150 Maquette for Wall Relief no. 2 *Bronze*
17¼ in. × 13 in. 1955 *Private Collection*

51 Maquette for Wall Relief no. 3 *Bronze*
4½ in. × 20½ in. 1955 *Private Collection*

52 Maquette for Wall Relief no. 9 *Bronze*
8½ in. × 13½ in. 1955 *Private Collection*

153 Studies for Standing Figures *Pencil, chalk and wash 23¼ in. × 19¼ in. 1951 Dr Andrew Revai, Pallas Gallery*

154 Metal Standing Figures *Chalk and watercolour*
$11\frac{1}{2}$ in. × $9\frac{1}{2}$ in. 1951 *Private Collection*

155 Three Standing Figures *Bronze 28 in.* 1953
Private Collection

truth is that painting and sculpture existed long before architecture was ever heard of. In Palaeolithic times, after all, men lived in caves, or in trees, and yet painting and sculpture were already going strong.

Just how Moore went on from there, in this and other cases, will be seen later. The immediate point is that in the first two maquettes (1952) for the Time-Life screen Moore used vertical elements in which he tried out all kinds of possible new figure-forms. Both schemes were dropped, however, for architectural reasons, and in the final draft the chunky, broad-based and partly transparent forms had a horizontal, as much as a vertical thrust, and all direct allusion to the human body was excluded.

The theme then seems to have gone underground until 1955, when it got going in a series of single figures, in a series of maquettes for a Wall Relief, and to a lesser extent in the large brick Wall Relief which was commissioned for the Bouwcentrum in Rotterdam. In none of these was it at all like the Vertical Figures of earlier days. The figure itself, as humanly constituted, had all but disappeared. Elements from it were arranged like an addition sum in mathematics. The top joint in each column did sometimes resemble the stylized Heads of 1953, or the Helmet Heads of a little earlier, and sometimes the bottom joint served as a pedestal. But fundamentally these were abstract arrangements that had a formal life of their own; a vigorous, versatile, all-purpose vitality that seemed to burst out of the columnar structure and set off all manner of associations. They were not so much reliefs, in the usual sense, as free-standing sculptures that seemed to have sunk into the body of the wall. Sometimes there was an echo of the 'fabulous animals' which he had set down in a sheet of drawings, and designated as such, the year before. Sometimes there were vegetable motives: a year or two earlier he had drawn a Reclining Figure of which the chest and belly were in the likeness of a pea-pod slit open up the middle. There were elements taken from machinery and from items of hardware: rings and screw-heads and graters. There were bone-forms and shell-forms imported entire with a freedom unknown since Moore's Surrealist days. There were complete fragments of a flattened architecture. There

156 Upright Motive no. 5 *Bronze 7 ft.* 1956 *Private Collection*

157 Upright Motive no. 3 *Bronze 10 in.* 1955 *Private Collection*

were reliefs in which the Vertical Figures stood
bolt upright, side by side, like a guard of honour,
and reliefs in which they seemed to have been
battened down out of sight. The more radical
and apparently disorganized (or perhaps merely
anti-organized) look of these pieces brought
Moore back to a position which he had earlier
vacated: that of a leader of the international
avant-garde. A piece like the *Wall Relief: Maquette
no. 6* of 1955 (pl. 149) has the unconditional,
take-it-or-leave-it quality that we associate with
Moore in the 1930s: and we remember that,
long before it was customary to accept such a
point of view, Moore was saying (in 1937, to be
exact) that 'if the work is to be more than a
sculptural exercise, unexplainable jumps in the
process of thought must occur'.

In these maquettes, the unity of the whole
overrides the individuality of the parts. But when
Moore came to make free-standing Vertical
Figures, he at times fell back into a neo
humanistic idiom that was basically that of the
little Stringed Figure of 1938: one or two even
retained stringed forms on the outside of
cylinder-like elements. Altered or 'perturbed'
objects, in the Surrealist sense, alternated in
these maquettes with sections that were like a
human torso writ small or one of the pebbles
worn through by water that had been among
Moore's favourite found objects in the 1930s.
There was a double problem to be solved: how
to bring to the abstract idiom of the Wall
Reliefs the unity and the meaningful articula-
tion of pieces based on the human figure; and
how to bring to that human figure the freedom
and the audacity and the manifold reverbera-
tion of the abstract idiom. Each extreme had
somehow to play up to the other and, by
sacrificing a part of its independence, be en-
hanced. Looking, for instance, at the *Glenkiln
Cross* which acts as leader of the *Three Upright
Motives,* we notice formal elements which go
straight back to the African wood *Torso* of 1927
(pl. 20). The smooth line from hip to shoulder
is one of these; another, the stylized knob which
stands for buttock and thigh. But in 1927 Moore
would not have known how to produce the
pedestal which merges almost imperceptibly
into the body above it: nor would he have
known how to wrench the top of the body into
that extraordinary gesture which gives it a
more-than-human thrust. The *Glenkiln Cross*

158 Upright Motive no. 4 *Bronze 11¼ in.* 1955
Marlborough Fine Art, New York

159 Upright Motive no. 9 *Bronze 10 in.* 1955
Marlborough Fine Art, New York

160 Upright Motive no. 7 *Bronze 12¼ in. 1955 Private Collection*

pl. 143) is one of Moore's greatest achievements: the figure itself man-size, the pedestal
hardly smaller, and the combination of the two
is arresting an image as has been created in
the twentieth century. Moore likened it to the
central image in the *Crucifixion*, when the three
pieces were set up together outside the Kröller-
Müller Museum in Otterlo; and, better than
many a specifically religious work of art, it can
bear the association. But it seems to me to lend
itself equally well to an affirmative interpretation. And the combination of the three Motives
does not seem to me necessarily to have anything to do with the *Crucifixion*. What to put
next to the *Glenkiln Cross* was certainly a great
problem, and one rendered all the harder by
the distinct human affinities of the *Cross*. But
Moore solved it by making the other two figures
that much less human. In them, the idiom
of the Wall Reliefs is carried out in three-
dimensional terms; and although there is a suggestion of a naturalistic torso, and the barest
implication of belly and pelvis and phallus and
rump, the pieces do not come within calling
distance of the *Glenkiln Cross* when it comes to
the identification of their elements. It is as if
Moore aimed, whether consciously or not, to
regain the ambiguity which the *Glenkiln Cross*
comes near to forfeiting. Seen together, the
three sculptures do not (to me, at any rate)
suggest a particular scene in history, august and
hallowed as that scene may be. They suggest a
gamut of feeling that runs from the tenderest of
human implications to the mere brute survival
of energies unconnected with our human designs. In doing this, they rejoin the central
tradition of twentieth-century art: instead of
illustrating what is already well known to us
from other sources, they formulate what has not
yet been put into words.

The *Three Upright Motives*, as set up at the
Kröller-Müller Museum, consist of no. 1 (the
Glenkiln Cross), no. 7 and no. 2. But there exist,
in all, twelve Upright Motives, though only five
got past the stage of the small maquette. Nos. 5
and 8 were cast at full scale (eighty-four and
seventy-eight inches high, respectively) and
they pursue the line of investigation represented
by no. 7 and no. 2. They do not, that is to say,
exploit the human figure directly, but what
looks at first sight like nozzle and slot could
equally well bear an anatomical interpretation;

and they attempt, also, to get away from the totem-pole principle, according to which isolated incidents can be piled one on top of another. They are recognizably striving towards a single coherent vertical form, even if they do not achieve it with the arresting immediacy of no. 1.

But, as happened with the Time-Life screen, the smaller maquettes have a lot to tell us about the auxiliary processes of Moore's imagination. No. 10, for instance, is basically a tower of bone or stone-forms, such as we have all made at some time on a beach: Moore has in his studio the materials for a hundred such towers. No. 8 has a beautifully worked and ornamented pedestal, and the topmost section is basically an armless torso. No. 9 takes the head off the torso and puts a much heavier emphasis on the naturalistic shoulders and breasts. Somewhere along the line Moore tried out and then discarded the idea of a straightforward column with a human body at the top of it: eddying between this and the free association of the Wall Relief maquettes, he did not quite clinch the one triumphant image of sexual exuberance which is struggling to get out in the series of Upright Motives. But in the graver vein of the *Glenkiln Cross* he succeeded absolutely.

Shortly after completing the Upright Motives Moore began on a venture which, though forecast in a number of wartime drawings, was quite new in sculpture. Those works which resulted consist, fundamentally, of figures in an environment. Moore has always resented the sculptor's helplessness in this matter, and the fact that the client, or the client's architect, can nullify the sculptor's intention without the sculptor having any redress – and, in fact, without his ever knowing anything about it.

Of course [he once said], one can't go on worrying about every piece one's done, and what's become of it, and whether it's well or badly shown. One's life would just be a misery. But sculpture does need more care in its placing than paintings do. With a picture, the frame keeps you at a distance and the picture goes on living in its own world. But if a sculpture is placed against the light, if you come into a room for instance and see it against the window, you just see a silhouette with a glare round it. It can't mean anything. If a thing is three-dimensional and meant to have a sense of complete existence it won't do to back it up against a wall like a child that's been put in the corner.

62 Three Upright Motives (including Glenkiln
Cross) *Bronze 10 ft. 6 in.* 1955–6 *Kröller-Müller Museum,
Otterlo; Amon Carter, Fort Worth, Texas*

158

158

158 Maquette for Wall Relief no. 7 *Plaster*
18¼ in. × 13¼ in. 1955 *Private Collection*

One way out of this is for the sculptor to be his own architect. Another is for the sculpture to carry its environment about with it: and this second solution is the basis of more than twenty pieces which Moore devised from 1956 onwards.

In some cases the environment is no more than a bench: but a bench so massive as to give dignity to whomever sits on it. Sometimes steps, rounded or square, support a seated figure. Sometimes the bench has a high curved back, or stands at right angles to a pitted wall, and sometimes the back is opened out, so that contrast and echo are established as between the figures and their background. Once the seated figure is set against an enormous structure that is more flattened throne than wall, and once or twice the environmental motif is combined with a return to the Draped Figure: these are some of the most popular of all Moore's pieces. By 1958–9 Moore had abandoned the use of the naturalistic figure, in this context, and was experimenting with sets of three Motives (*presences* might be a better word) against a wall. The first of these (pl. 165) makes use of anatomical

motifs: but no. 2, completed in 1959, dispense. not only with the benches and pedestals of the earlier work but with all overt allusion to the human form. As with some of the Uprigh Motive maquettes, Moore has gone back to the animal-cum-mineral forms which abound in hi studio, and the combination of these cryptic and sinister objects with a blind, prison-like wall is one of his most arresting inventions Moore himself has always refused, as I said earlier, to hitch himself to any of the grea dramatists of the spoken or the lyric stage; bu when we have studied the environmental serie from beginning to end it seems natural tha Wieland Wagner should have drawn upor Moore's imagery, as he avowedly did, for hi production of *The Ring* at Bayreuth in 1965 (Victor Gollancz reported on this as follows 'The dominant influence, as Herr Wieland acknowledged, is Henry Moore. I would men tion in particular the spiky backcloth for *Sieg fried*, Act II; the crater-pitted castle in *Gotterdämmerung*; and above all the immensel powerful picture for *Die Walküre*, Act II, wit

ts great holes, and its clash of verticals and
horizontals jutting out in a sort of steel-blue
hale.')

We have no warrant whatever for regarding
Moore's as a Wagnerian genius, but in two
respects his art does at moments run parallel to
Wagner's. In both, the idea of landscape
appears as something august and terrible,
while architecture is pre-eminently a department of admonition. Moore produced his most
elaborate essay of this kind in *The Wall: Background for Sculpture*, 1962 (pl. 168). At first this
looks like a piece of latter-day landscaping:
something that Batty Langley might have produced if he had read Kafka. But if we look
again, Bayreuth does seem the right place. Even
more remarkable in its way is the *Large Torso:
Arch* of 1962–3: architecture here *is* the human
body. Actually to walk through this piece is a
curious experience. On one level, it offers the
total involvement for which many of Moore's
larger pieces seem to call. On another, it is a
gesture of defiance towards architecture, as if
the artist were saying that in several thousand

years the idea of the triumphal arch had not
been more solemnly exemplified than in this
sculpture, which owes as much to the charnel-
house as to Vitruvius.

Moore is comparable to Wagner also in his
command of animal forms which, without belonging to established mythology, could take
their place in it as if by right. (And not of
animal forms only, for that matter: who better
than Moore could devise the magic helmet in
Rheingold, or Mime's forge, or Brunnhilde's
rock, or the Ring itself?) Over and over again
in the 1950s and 1960s Moore has invented
animal-forms which belong to no known
bestiary and yet are quintessentially plausible.
We can't give a name to them, but we accept
the fact of their existence. Moore's art is at its
most powerful, as I see it, when these evocations
overlap with human presences. A piece like the
Three-quarter Figure of 1961 (pl. 170), or even
more so the *Three-part Object* of 1960, is a re-
minder of unsubdued forces within us. These
owe allegiance not to one particular creature –
lion, hyena, tiger, jackal, elephant, vulture –

165 Three Motives against Wall no. 1 *Bronze*
42 in. × 18½ in. 1958–9 Private Collection

166 Definitive maquette for Bouwcentrum Wall
Bronze 22½ in. × 10 in. 1955 Private Collection

that we could name with respect or abhorrence, but to an anonymous residue, a mindless persistence and blind ingenuity that we have not yet classified. Even the *Slow Form: Tortoise* of 1962 (pl. 172), which for once has a title precise enough even for the zoo, has characteristics that would baffle Buffon. And as for the *Three-part Object*, even Moore himself has always refused to say, or perhaps to investigate, what it is really about.

It has a sort of animal/vegetable mixture [he once said]. It's not human, but neither is it animal or vegetable. Well, I just don't know how it came about. I don't know how a piece like that begins. I just begin in the morning with a bit of plaster or a bit of clay and a form comes about. Either it has some interest, and keeps it, or it doesn't. If it has, I go on without having to know, or trying to know, exactly what it means. I wish in a way that I could be even freer than I am from the tie of having to know exactly what it means, so that I could take a form and develop it and carry it further without ever having to have an 'explanation'.

And there is no doubt that it is the anarchical imagination that has kept Moore's art from ever settling down. Something in him keeps up the long steady swing between the sweet reasonableness of the Rocking-chair piece of 1950 (pl. 174) and the snouted, misshapen, dwarfish creatures that stand for the night-side of an artist whom people associate, on the whole quite rightly, with the broad and open light of day. Our generation has outgrown the idea of monsters – which is one reason why naturalistic Wagnerian production had to come to a halt – but there are also monsters that we have not yet grown up to: and Moore is one of the men who can make them.

The element of the unsubdued imagination runs right through Moore's work in the 1950s and 1960s. Public bodies are not very fond of it, because it leads to work which does not correspond to any established image of Moore. People who commission a sculpture like to get 'the same again, only more so', and I don't doubt that sighs of relief were heard when it became known in the mid 1950s that for the new UNESCO building in Paris Moore had

167 Three Motives against Wall no. 2 *Bronze*
42 in. × 15 in. 1959 Private Collection

168 The Wall: Background for Sculpture *Bronze*
8 ft. 4 in. × 7 ft. 1962 Artist's Collection

169 Large Torso: Arch *Bronze 6 ft. 9½ in. × 4 ft. 2 in.*
1962 *Dr W. Stahelin, Zürich*

170 Three-quarter Figure *Bronze 15 in.* 1961 *Private Collection*

171 Three-part Object *Bronze 48½ in.* 1960 *Private Collection*

172 Slow Form (Tortoise) *Bronze length 8½ in.* 1962 *Private Collection*

chosen to do a reclining figure. The motif of the reclining figure has, in fact, been treated with a signal ruthlessness throughout Moore's career. But there is a basic majesty about the idea of a huge woman lying down that is in itself reassuring: and there was reassurance also in the news that Moore was going to Carrara for his material. Italy has the effect, broadly speaking, of domesticating the subversive element in Moore's art. Carving is a long, slow, steady, ruminative process that rules out, almost by definition, the darting and insubordinate insights which find outlet in his small bronzes. Everything pointed, therefore, to the emergence of something that could be related in general terms to the ultimate object of UNESCO's activities: exalted relaxation, that is to say.

Moore does not, of course, subscribe to the view that because a figure is lying down it is necessarily going to enjoy itself. 'Alerted' was his adjective for the state of mind of the Time-Life figure, and a generalized vigilance, an anxiety just held in check, is the note of many of the pre-war Reclining Figures. He regards the subject, moreover, as one capable of ever imaginable nuance of expression.

Sometimes an artist has a set theme that he take over and over again – Cézanne and his bathers ar a case in point – and the theme frees him to try ou all sorts of things that he doesn't quite know o isn't quite sure of. With me, the reclining figur offers that kind of chance. The subject is settled fo one, one knows it and likes it, and therefore one' free to make a new form-idea within that subjec that may be completely different from any othe idea that one's ever had. The subject-matter free one, and yet it gives what one does a continuity...

The UNESCO figure is the latest and th largest (200 inches in length) of Moore's carv ings, and it is in a material – Roman Travertin marble – that means a great deal to him. Th block came from a quarry that Michelangel had used; and, quite apart from the idea c continuity which this represented, Moore wa stirred by the exceptional scale of the quarryin operations – the blocks as big as a house tha were manœuvred down the mountain-side, an

73 Reclining Figure (maquette for UNESCO sculpture) *Bronze length 8¼ in. 1956 Private Collection*

he strange involuntary poetry of the photographs in the quarry-master's office.

There was one huge block – as big as this room urned on end and twice as high – and a ladder vith a man perched on the top of it, and in one orner a man's bowler hat, a hat of about 1900, I hould think, and this hat and the ladder and the nan at the top of it combined to give one a sense of dmost unbelievable scale and reminded me of the ind of things that I could try to get out of the lock. . . .

When we last looked at undraped Reclining igures in this book, two main tendencies were sserting themselves. One is the sense of drawing 1 the air that comes out strongest in the figure f 1951 (pl. 123): here the empty spaces are as nportant as the thing drawn in bronze. The ther is the sense of enclosed space that comes ut in the reclining Internal and External gure of 1951. Here, too, the empty spaces re as important as the forms which surround nd define them, but the psychological situa-on is a great deal more complex: whether the

interior is prison or sanctuary, womb or detested cage, is a question that the artist leaves open. It remained in abeyance while Moore worked on the Time-Life draped figure, and at the time of the warriors, the *King and Queen*, and the Harlow *Family Group*, it just didn't arise: conceivably the tensions which it provoked were too great to be managed at the moment and had to go underground.

It was unlikely, in any case, and for several reasons, that problems of this sort would be tackled in the UNESCO figure. Everyone is entitled to his opinion of the activities of UNESCO, but its foundation was pre-eminently a constructive, not to say an optimistic gesture; and one which took for granted the perfectibility of the post-war world. Time may have blown upon this notion, but it remains one to which the externalization of private dramas, no matter how universal, would be inappropriate. The problem of the UNESCO figure was, in short, the problem of how to make a Promised-Land figure without resorting to Promised-Land art. Erich Neumann put this in more scientific

174 Rocking Chair no. 2 *Bronze 11 in.* 1950 *Private Collection*

erms when he spoke of Moore's having helped, with his Reclining Figures, to 'activate a feminine archetype' which would offset the one-sided patriarchal culture' which characterizes the Western world in the twentieth century. The birth of the feminine archetype in modern man', he said, 'signifies at the same time the development of human relatedness, of his social capacity, and the growing consciousness of the unity of mankind on earth.' Herbert Read was on the right lines, surely, when he quoted this passage and said that Moore's Reclining Figure, thus interpreted, ideally symbolized the aims of UNESCO.

During the period of cogitation Moore experimented with a large number of subjects that were loosely related to the UNESCO problem: Mothers and Children, Family groups, single figures seated or standing in front of a wall, and so on. Some of these were later cast in bronze, but none of them, in the end, would have done for his purpose. For one thing, the sculpture had to stand against a background of fenestration which looks mathematical in a scale-model

but in life tends to be fussy and chaotic. The light on the windows themselves, and on the lattices of support and balcony, gets glary and irritable if the weather is at all fine. The green of the surrounding grass must also be taken into account.

All this put bronze out of account and made out of the question, also, a piece that depended on intimacy and nuance. (The visitor is not allowed to approach within twenty or thirty yards of the sculpture.) White marble and plain statement were the thing: white marble to combat the fuss and glare of the building itself, plain statement to serve as a mascot for activities which begin as a department of a holy war and all too often end as a department of international tax-free bureaucracy. The bronze *Working Model* for the UNESCO figure is an affair of dramatic shadows, of light glimpsed through darkness, of great louring fell-like hollows and heights: a northerly piece, if ever there was one. Transposed into Roman Travertine marble, those same tunnels take on the likeness of a road cut through the southern flank

176 Reclining Figure *Roman Travertine 17 ft.* 1957
UNESCO Building, Paris

177 Draped Reclining Woman *Bronze 6 ft. 10 in.*
1957 *Sir Robert Sainsbury, London*

of the Alps, and those same clefts and over-hanging bluffs the likeness of a cavern by the sea in Homer. The upward thrust of leg and shoulder is balanced by delicate black horizontal markings in the marble. The striations on the back of the head, which look in the bronze like the marks of hard weathering, look in the marble like incisions in material blanched by salt winds and Aegean sunshine. This dexterous alliance of north and south is one of the happiest features of a piece which has just the weight, and just the quality of 'pull', to detach it cleanly and for ever from its background. The UNESCO figure has never had the Press it deserves – French critics in particular and French opinion in general can never bear to give credit to British art – but to me it seems to be the right answer to an impossible question.

That answer was given, as I indicated, in terms of Moore's public manner. Nothing in the piece could be said to contest the central tenet of UNESCO: that if human nature is given the right opportunities it will get better and better. Moore himself is steadfast and affectionate in private relations and has something of the constructive optimism of the school-masters from whom he learned so much at the start of his life. But, as Proust points out in *Against Sainte-Beuve*, the self which produces work of art is a different self altogether from the self which comes out in life. Nothing is more instructive, in this context, than to compare the maquettes which Moore produced in 1956–7 when he was trying out one idea after another for the UNESCO piece, with the related work which he produced in 1957–8, when the UNESCO problem was out of the way. The earlier group is pacific in tone and naturalistic in idiom: somewhere within each of them is the idea of the Good Family, the Good Mother, the Good Individual, and the Good Society. The attitudes of the individual figures are those of the sage counsellor, the well-trained son or daughter, the husband and wife caught at a moment of quiet communion. But once duty had been done, and been seen to be done, the tusky and unregenerate side of Moore's art made itself felt again.

It made itself felt, what is more, in precisely the terms of the UNESCO maquettes. The wall was there, and the standing or seated figures, and the bench that might have served for some village parliament. But in the *Three Motives against Wall no. 1* (pl. 165) of 1958 the three figures were in retreat from humanity, and in the *Three Motives against Wall no. 2* of 1959 they had lost touch with it altogether. There could be no clearer illustration of the tendency of Moore's imagination, when left to itself, to veer away from the classical approach of European humanism and tack towards the demonic forces implicit in the animal and vegetable kingdoms, in the millennial workings of boulder and rock-face, and in the idioms of non-European art. In the *Three Motives, no. 1* the figure on the left is perceptibly the cousin of the seated figures in the UNESCO maquettes; the central figure derives from the found objects of the 1930s but is still recognizably human in its derivation, and the figure on the right is like a reclining figure up-ended and poised in the attitude of a dinosaur in an Edwardian boys' magazine.

Each has its podium, and together they look like first, second, and third in a space-fiction Olympiad, with electronic national anthems somewhere unheard. But in the *Three Motives, no. 2* the podiums have been whipped away and the three anonymous, unnameable forms are just *there*: no explanation comes to hand. Anyone who has watched a space-fiction serial will know that the most difficult thing is to carry conviction with an invented form that does not somewhere rely upon human or mechanical affinities. Moore has achieved, here, what the novelist and scenarist fall down on: the invention of forms which impress themselves immediately as definable personalities and yet do not appeal to already existing categories of experience. And they carry conviction as a group, moreover: there really is a relationship between them as individuals, and as members of a group, and between them and their environment. The scene is the scene, unchanged, of many of Moore's wartime drawings; but another race now inhabits it.

Moore was to tack back again towards a

179 Draped Reclining Woman (detail) *Bronze*
6 ft. 10 in. 1957 Sir Robert Sainsbury, London

world of legible anatomies. In 1960 the *Two Seated Girls Against Wall*, and in the same year the *Seated Figure: Arms Outstretched*, have a freedom of reference which can be traced to the *Three Motives against Wall, nos. 1 and 2.* But the basic advantage of absolute autonomy – the right, that is to say, to push forward independently of all sentimental allusion to the heroic art of the past – was never quite forfeited again. Moore began, also, to make private images on a public scale. By casting these in bronze, and in editions of six or more, he was able to gain for them a wider currency than had been possible with the unique pieces of the 1930s and 1940s. It soon came about, in fact, that public collections overseas thought of Moore primarily in terms of the large bronzes of the 1950s and 1960s; and he could have gone on with the big neo-Classical draped figures in much the same way as Maillol went on with his full-breasted and bull-bottomed peasant girls. They were as acceptable to the San Francisco Longshoremen's Union, which wanted to commission a bronze, as to the Trustees of Yale University Art Gallery. Basically these are undemanding pieces which give enormous pleasure: the *Draped Seated Woman* of 1957–8 has, for instance, a vespertinal look, a ripeness like that of Richard Strauss's 'Four Last Songs': with its contemporary the *Draped Reclining Woman* it induces a feeling of unfocused regret, and anyone who has seen either piece in the open, in an environment of dark trees and falling water, will know that as symbols of withdrawal they would be difficult to excel.

But withdrawal is not a characteristic of Moore, any more than passivity is a characteristic of his major figures. Moore's women at their best abrogate to themselves the masculine qualities of power, determination, authority, and endurance, and they become, as Michelangelo said of Vittoria Colonna, 'un uomo in una donna, anzi uno dio'. When he had got free of the UNESCO commission he gave the tender side of his nature free rein in the two Draped Figures; but these arose directly from trial runs for the UNESCO figure and from the momentum of Moore's efforts in that direction: nothing was more reasonable than that Moore should make use of material which, though unsuited to the UNESCO building, has given intense satisfaction elsewhere. But, as happened with the *Three Motives against a Wall*, the tough side of his nature broke out with all the more ferocity for having been so long kept out of sight: 1959–61 was to be a period of exceptional activity on that account.

There had been portents of a return to the woman-as-superman theme. In 1956 an eight-foot-long Reclining Figure in bronze had come as near as Moore had ever come to the exaggerations of Expressionism: movement and attitude were heightened for expressive effect and the figure seemed to be heaving itself out of the mould, just as in the Reclining Figures of the 1920s the female animal gazed out at us as if to say that she was trapped as much by the fatality of the block as by any external predicament. In the *Upright Figure* in elmwood of 1956–60 (pls. 181, 182), which went to the Guggenheim Museum before it was ever shown in England, this theme was up-ended and the figure seems to be struggling as much to get free of the wall as to climb up it. In both cases the idiom itself was unusually cautious for Moore as if he were for once not quite certain how far to push the idea. By 1959 every doubt had vanished: 'all the way' was the answer. In the monumental *Relief, no. 1* the human body is seen as something robust as a rhino: with something, in fact, of a rhino's armoured hide, and something of its power to trample and thrust when and where we least expect it. To imagine what movements might aptly be forthcoming from this tremendous creature we should turn rather to Wilhelm Reich on the orgasm than to any manual of the classical dance. Old-style aestheticizing, and considerations of 'beauty' and 'ugliness' are meaningless in the context of this relief. It is, understandably, one of the least popular of his pieces: and nothing could give more conclusive proof of Moore's vitality as an artist than his ability to produce a commandingly powerful work which almost nobody likes.

Moore turned his mind, at the same time, to the renewal of the Reclining Figure. He had come to maturity at a time when there was still something startling and provocative in the idea of the kinship between human forms and those of vegetable or mineral origin. Moore raided landscape, also, for certain qualities of roundness and smoothness. And he used materials, at that stage, which were predominantly sleek for all the toughness of the ideas behind them.

184, 185, 186 Reclining Figure *Elmwood length 7 ft. 6 in.*
1959–64 *Artist's Collection*

187 and 188 Two-piece Reclining Figure no. 1
Bronze length 76 in. 1959 *Albright-Knox Art Gallery, Buffalo*

here is an inexpugnable elegance about many of the pre-war carvings. The sinews remained fine, no matter how rugged was the artist's intention. But ever since the Upright Motives of 1955 Moore had dropped this fineness of sinew, had got out of the drawing-room, one might say, and into – what? The sacrificial pen? A forbidden temple? Or the Pantheon of some race heavier in limb, and more resistant in spirit, than our own?

The two- and three-piece Reclining Figures of 1959–62 are the pieces which count in this context. Throughout the period in question Moore was at work, also, on the elmwood *Reclining Figure* (pls. 184, 185, 186) which he began in 1959 and finished only five years later; and this very beautiful piece is relevant to the others in so far as, in contrast to them, it relies on the continuous line. Looking at it, we can gaze in perpetuity: never is the eye brought up short. This is a consolidatory work, related back to the Onslow-Ford figure of just before the war; but it has a steady, unbroken coherence, a regular persistent exploration of a given idea, which are

the more striking in contrast to the two- and three-piece Reclining Figures. For these are portraits of Upheaval; and their architecture is an architecture of survival and not, as in many earlier Reclining Figures, of consolation. What they stand for, fundamentally, is the ability of the human body to survive and dominate, no matter how catastrophic its surroundings. Fragmentary and ruinous as is the condition of these huge carcasses, their aspect is not one of collapse. Never are they merely inert. On the contrary: the upraised leg in *Two-piece Reclining Figure no. 1* is probably the most dynamic incident in all Moore's work: nor has the watch-tower of the head ever been more regally poised.

In most of the Reclining Figures with which sculpture has endowed us, certain areas sustain our interest at a greater level of intensity than others. But in these large late figures by Moore no one part, and no one view, is more compelling than the others. They are works that must be toured, not quizzed; lived in, not visited; read from end to end, and not encapsulated. The student must see their seasons round before

189 and 190 Two-piece Reclining Figure no. 2
Bronze length 8 ft. 6 in. 1960 Tate Gallery, London

191 and 192 Two-piece Reclining Figure no. 3
Bronze length 7 ft. 10 in. 1961 Gothenburg, Sweden

e can claim to know them. For the ferocity of their inspiration they are paralleled by the *Three Upright Motives* of 1955–6. Each of those totem-like figures has a single climax, to which the eye is led: all is coherent, one-minded, taut. But in the two-piece Reclining Figures Moore can afford to let our attention wander at will: what does not come in with one tide will come in with the next.

The tidal image is not chosen at random. If these pieces have any one single secondary significance, it is that of an eroded coast. Photography brings this out better than words; but if Walter Pater were to come back to earth and see one of these figures he would not say of it, as he said of the *Mona Lisa*, that she was 'older than the rocks among which she sits': he would see that she *was* those rocks. Rock and woman are one, in these pieces: it is as if the famous cliff-structure near Étretat, which played so large a part in French late nineteenth-century painting, had become a metaphor for the human body. To this effect the special nature of bronze contributes: in fact I doubt if the dogged, sullen quality of a very large bronze cast has ever been used more cunningly. Bronze has, as much as alabaster, its load of connotations from the past. (This is one of the reasons why it has been rejected with such absolute scorn by many sculptors of the younger generation.) And the problem for a sculptor is to get those connotations to work for him and not against him. The observer must not say, 'That's very good, but after all Rodin did it better.' Nor, at this stage in the history of art, is the weight and bulk of bronze anything but a handicap: '*Aere perennius* my foot!' would be our generation's reply to Horace if he ever got off that Sabine farm. What counted as plus for so long now counts as minus: bronze is, in fact, in the situation that the nineteenth-century cathedral organ was in before Messiaen came along to write for it. Messiaen redeemed that organ by taking the characteristics which had put people off and pushing them so far that he came out, as it were, on the other side. And Moore does something of the same in the two- and three-piece Reclining Figures. What people dislike in bronze is the mandatory solemnity, the trombone-voice that says, 'Hats off! This is Art.' Bronze-casting is believed, too, to produce something that is a translation, if not a blurred approximation, of

the original sculptural idea. This may be true, or it may be a misreading of the caster's role, and a misreading, also, of the sculptor's ability to allow for these approximations and, even, to exploit them as each cast comes back from the founder. But, whether right or wrong, it is the reason, or a large part of the reason, why young artists have turned to materials which are light, and can be coloured at will, and have nothing to do with high art.

What Moore did, in these large figures, can be studied in photographs; and very imposing some of his own photographs are. We see at once how, so far from smoothing away the working-marks of the original plaster, Moore has emphasized them in the finished bronze. The basic texture of these pieces is not 'expressive' in the way that a bronze by Rodin or Matisse or Giacometti is expressive. Moore is intent, on the contrary, on keeping 'expressiveness' at a distance. This is not because he disapproves of it (no one is more loyal to bronze) but because he does not want the observer to slip into aestheticizing.

Photographs can show this, as I say. But nothing substitutes for the experience of walking all round these pieces. The *Two-piece Reclining Figure no. 2* has, for instance, been on loan from the Arts Council to the Scottish National Gallery of Modern Art in Edinburgh. Placed on the lawn at the top of the Royal Botanical Garden, with a view that stretches across Princes Street, across the New Town, and away to the mountains beyond, it makes an astonishing effect. For once the mountains in the piece and the mountains in 'real life' are allowed to harmonize. We realize all over again that what Moore has produced is an imaginary landscape that happens to relate at every point to the human body, to human emotional states, and to aspects of human experience. We wonder afresh at the mysterious three-way tunnels – impossible, these, to photograph – which characterize both halves of the piece. Edinburgh weather, so impulsive and imperious, so rich in short-term incident, is somehow called to order by a piece that maintains its own tempo and simply will not be hurried into registering every whim of the elements. And in all this the basic unit of expression is that of the marks made on a rock-face by the climber's axe, or on a coal-face by the miner's pick: Moore nowhere relies

193 and 194 Reclining Mother and Child *Bronze*
7 ft. 2½ in. 1960 Walker Art Center, Minneapolis

on the traditional idiom of plaster transmuted into bronze.

Moore originally hit on the two-piece idea when he found that a clean break somewhere in the middle opened up possibilities of tension and antithesis, statement and counter-statement, which simply could not be explored within a single form. The reader can judge of this for himself by imagining the two-piece Reclining Figures with the central gap filled in: the sculpture at once becomes unintelligible. Here again, no photograph can convey the impact of the empty space as it reveals itself when we walk round either end of the figure. Somewhere within that impact is the idea of irreparable separation and loss which is fundamental to all human experience; and art's highest function is fulfilled when we look again and realize that the two pieces have an intense and living relationship, as separate entities, which would be dulled and rendered inert if they were to be joined together.

The idea of the divided piece was not, of course, a new one. Moore did, as we have seen, make several sculptures in two, three, and four pieces in the 1930s. What was new was the scale of the works: the fact that it was as much a bodily as a merely ocular experience to get to grips with them. New, also, was the texture: working on so large a scale, Moore could afford to reject the smoothness of the 1930s, and in fact to lose the image altogether, in the confidence that the overall design was grand enough to pull the observer through. Clearly it was only a matter of time before he made a figure in three pieces, as well as in two; and in 1962 he did produce a small maquette that broke new ground, even if it did tread it rather uncertainly. In style this was midway between the landscape idea of the big two-piece Reclining Figures (the legs and feet, for instance) and the 1930-ish object-of-art (the head and shoulders). It was highly polished, also, and in between the two pieces I have characterized here was a third element that derived from the bone-forms of earlier years. But when the large *Three-piece Reclining Figure* of 1961-2 (pl. 196) came along it was in the landscape-idiom of the large two-piece Reclining Figures: like them, it made a great effect of monumentality by rejecting the means which normally conduce to monumentality. It did not, that is to say, rely on the rhetoric of familiar forms; nor did it aim at any one obvious climax. If anything, the forms were even more closely related to cliff-face and mountain-side than were those of the four earlier figures. Human anatomy, recognizably the point of departure for the two-piece Reclining Figures, was getting farther and farther away: and *The Wall* of 1962 (pl. 168) was getting nearer. It was difficult to see that this particular line of effort could be pushed further, more especially as the idiom was one which relied to a certain extent on the sensations of surprise and disorientation with which we felt our way round the first two or three pieces. One could put this very briefly and crudely by saying that in the 1930s Moore made the point that human beings could look like boulders; in the late 1950s he made the point that boulders could look like human beings; and at the beginning of the 1960s he was beginning to make the point that boulders look like boulders: very imposing and finely-worked boulders, but boulders none the less. Something of the pull of opposites was being lost, although the scenic element – the sensations brought into being when an observer walked slowly right round the piece – was grander than ever.

Another artist might, in these circumstances, have run aground in a welter of picturesque landscaping. Cliffs ever more horrendous, caverns ever more serpentine, bluffs ever more meaningfully knobbed and pocked, might have taken the place of genuine inspiration: it would have been like starting with *Oedipus at Colonus* and ending up with the Gothick novel. But already with the *Two-piece Reclining Figure no. 3* of 1961 (pl. 192), there were portents of a new evolution. The butt-end of that piece was a matter not of landscaping, but of thrusts paralleled, surely, in architecture and, even more, in engineering. Ever since Le Corbusier pioneered the idea of a city of stilts, architecture has meditated the notion of great masses lifted clear of the ground. The bridge, in particular, is a form of construction in which the late nineteenth and twentieth centuries have excelled: a form, also, which more than most architectural inventions approximates to sculpture. So it seems only natural that the last Reclining Figure in this book should derive in large part from engineering forms. The *Three-piece Reclining Figure no. 2: Bridge Prop* of 1963 differs from

195 Three-piece Reclining Figure no. 2: Bridge
Prop *Bronze length 8 ft. 3 in. 1963 City Art Gallery
and Museum, Leeds*

196 Three-piece Reclining Figure *Bronze length*
9 ft. 6 in. 1961–2 *National Bank of Canada, Montreal*

the earlier two- and three-piece figures in that its forms are sharply defined, owe nothing to the poetry of near-dereliction, and present the human body in terms that look forward to a heroic, or at any rate to a serviceable future, instead of looking back to a past in which to have come through was in itself an achievement. The Bridge Prop figure is, in fact, a raid upon the preserves of post-war architecture. In eschewing so firmly the pathos of the earlier multiple figures, and in choosing forms which had a minimum of direct emotional appeal, Moore once again broke free from the successes of his immediate past. Younger sculptors think it very grand and daring to make use of ready-made industrial sections, but Moore's achievement in the Bridge Prop piece is that he invented sections which have the same look of functional efficiency and are yet unmistakably his own. We should not be surprised if we went into a ship-chandler's, or into a repair shop underneath the Forth Bridge, and found any one of the three components of this sculpture lying around ready for some specific use: and yet, when put together, they make a metaphor for an exceptionally powerful and resourceful human being. What happened with the draped figures has happened once again: Moore has broken free in good time.

VII SINCE 1963

Moore in the 1960s has been exploring a great many ideas, and he has left himself free to take them up and put them down as suits him best. For instance the natural pair and pendant to the Bridge Prop piece of 1963 is the *Two-piece: Pipe*, where the nonchalant pose of the bridge prop is transposed in erotic terms. But the *Two-piece: Pipe* is dated 1966. Equally, the bronze of 1959 called *Mother and Child: Hollow* harks back to the vigils and alarms of 1929–30; the *Two Torso* (*Maquette*) of 1962 is a late homage to Rodin; and the *Thin Figure* of 1965 is the kind of delicately characterized piece which relates rather to sixteenth-century Italian bronzes than to any 'coherent' account of Moore's evolution. Other recent pieces are late variants of themes which keep coming back and back into Moore's awareness: the *Helmet Heads* (no. 4, 1963, and no. 5 (Giraffe), 1966) and the little *Reclining Interior* (*Oval*), 1965.

Pieces like these keep the sculptor's private imagination alive. But Moore in the 1960s is continually being honoured (or plagued, according to one's point of view) by requests for major public statements. It is not always easy on such occasions to distinguish between the job which might fulfil the ambition of a lifetime and the job which fundamentally represents a disguised philistinism on the part of those who suggest it. Large-scale commissions are subject to all manner of small disappointments. (At the Lincoln Center in New York, for instance, the level of the water round the huge Moore *Reclining Figure* is rarely or never as the artist intended.) Yet there are challenges which a man of spirit will find it difficult to refuse: one such was the invitation from the Lincoln Center, and another the commission from Chicago for a piece which would commemorate the work done there on atomic physics.

In the Lincoln Center piece, Moore took the opportunity of completing once and for all the experience which had begun with the Two-Piece Reclining Figures of 1959–60. As time went on, and Moore himself was able to stand aside from these works, their sources became more and more clear. Moore has spoken of two paintings which contributed to them – Seurat's *Bec du Hoc* in the National Gallery, and Monet's *Cliffs at Étretat, 1883* in the Metropolitan Museum – by their evocation of natural forms hollowed out or up-ended; he has also been reminded of the Adle Rock, not far from his birthplace, which he first saw in 1908 or thereabouts and

198 Two-piece Sculpture: Pipe *Bronze length 37 in.*
1966 *Whitworth Art Gallery, Manchester*

had harboured in his imagination ever since. I also think, though I have no warrant for saying so, that something in the present state of the Elgin Marbles may have made a contribution. Group after group in the British Museum survives in fragmented and eroded shape, with an unintended vacancy where once the forms were in close and majestic communication. But that very break in the forms turns out to have an expressiveness of its own; and this expressiveness recurs, as it seems to me, in Moore's two- and three-piece Reclining Figures. That the Elgin Marbles should one day serve as metaphors for survival was certainly no part of Pheidias' intention; nor did Moore plan to provide the pleasure-bound New Yorker with a spurious antiquity. Big works of art are big enough to stand up to all manner of interpretations – if this were not so, the free-thinker would feel uneasy at *The Magic Flute* – and they are not at all diminished if we happen to stumble on one of the elements which went to their making. We do not think less of *The Polish Rider* because Rembrandt may have had in mind a generalized image of the *miles Christianus* and could have filched his composition from a reversed version of the knight in Dürer's *Knight, Death, and Devil*. Rembrandt's artistic personality was strong enough to make these borrowings into something of his own. Similarly – and without making comparisons which Moore would be the first to discard – the Lincoln Center piece is strong enough to digest both Pheidias *and* the Adle, both Monet's *Cliffs at Étretat and* the experience of Étretat itself, and doubtless a great many other ingredients among everything that Moore has experienced. The cantilever-like thrust of the torso is, in particular, one of his most forceful images.

The *Atom Piece* is something different again. Initially, Moore was not attracted by the idea of celebrating an activity which in many of its aspects has brought us little but foreboding. Memorials as such seem to him an outmoded use for sculpture, and this particular subject did not prompt him to change his mind. But when he came to think about it at length he found that a certain specific form did suggest itself, and that this form was relevant both to the set subject and to his own inmost preoccupations. So he went ahead: and the piece which resulted is an amalgam of many congruent ideas – among them the profile of the human cranium, the outline of the mushroom-cloud, the notion of the armoured head as it is often found in Moore's work, and the idea of the inward-outward form which is at once fortress and prison. There was also a tension quite new in Moore's work: that between the rugosities natural to bronze and the suavity of marble. This tension manifests itself as between the upper part of the piece – the bald, seamless cranium – and the pocked and weathered-looking base.

I have no warrant for my opinion, but I suspect that this polarity derives from the fact that in recent years Moore has renewed his contacts with the world of direct carving. Not long after he was awarded the Feltrinelli Prize in 1963, Moore went house-hunting in Italy. He settled in the end for a little house in the flatlands just north of Forte dei Marmi. From his garden he can look up to the Carrara Mountains, and in particular to the quarries now worked by Messrs Henraux. These lie in the stretch of mountain in which Michelangelo is said to have gone in search of stone, and the topmost workings are to this day as impressive a scene as can be found anywhere in Italy. One would have, in fact, to go to Delphi itself to find somewhere more directly suggestive of the home of the gods. Not only are the mountains themselves irresistibly grand, with their shifting cloudscapes and sudden daunting fits of ill-humour, but the enormous concealed caverns of marble form a scene to silence even the most reckless among us. It is as if we were whisked back, literally, to the Stone Age: man and matter are confronted, and the raw materials of art present themselves as nowhere else.

It is one of the fatalities of an inept society that these materials are put mostly to uses quite unworthy of them. But an artist with Moore's sensitivity to material could not in such circumstances fail to fall in love all over again with the potentialities of stone. It was a year or two before he actually got down to direct carving

200 DANESE CATTENEO Allegory of Vanity,
or The Negro Venus *Bronze Heim Gallery*

201 Thin Figure *Plaster 8 in.* 1965 *Cast in 1968*

203 Helmet Head no. 4 *Bronze 18¾ in.* 1963 *Private
Collection*

204 Reclining Interior (Oval) *Bronze 8 in.* 1965
Private Collection

205 and 206 Reclining Figure (working model for
Lincoln Center sculpture) *Bronze length 14 ft.* 1963
Mr and Mrs Albert List, New York

again; but I do not believe that it was coincidence that led him, from 1962 onwards, to concentrate more and more on surfaces that were smooth and unbroken and edges that were sharp and clean.

This shift of interest had a double source. After a long period in which bronze casts dominated his imagination Moore was quite ready for their antithesis. He found this in another lifelong preoccupation: bones. 'Since my student days', he wrote in 1962, 'I have liked the shape of bones and have drawn them, studied them in the Natural History Museum, found them on sea-shores and saved them out of the stew-pot.' It also happens that part of his garden in the country once belonged to a butcher, and that old bones are constantly being turned up there. Moore's interest in bones goes, moreover, far beyond the fact that their forms are suggestive.

There are [he says], many structural and sculptural principles to be learned from bones, e.g. that in spite of their lightness they have great strength.

Some bones, such as the breast-bones of birds, have the lightweight fineness of a knife-blade. . . . In 1961 I used this knife-edged thinness throughout a whole figure, the *Standing Figure (Knife-edge)*.

Moore himself has suggested that there may be something of the Louvre *Victory of Samothrace* in this figure; this gives it a place midway in the transition from those larger pieces for which an august cousinage can be claimed to the late carvings which for the most part defy such analysis. We believe in bones as a prime source of the *Standing Figure (Knife-edge)*, and we can see their influence on a piece like the *Knife-edge (two-piece)* 1962; but in the later piece there is already, I think, a distinct allusion to the experience of the stone-yard. Anyone who has spent a morning at Henraux's will have noticed that by lunch-time there is something compelling about the cutting and slicing, as such, of the stone. It matters hardly at all that the ends are those of everyday funerary sculpture: what matters is the means. This applies as much to the hammer and chisel which have one man's

arm behind them as it does to the redoubtable, screeching, invincible powered saw. The unambiguous light also plays a part in persuading us that this is a language in which everything is brought out into the open. The sonorous equivocations of bronze are forgotten as we stand in awe before material that has come down from the throne-room of the gods and can never be totally degraded.

Perhaps one should also bear in mind the fact that a great many supremely beautiful pieces of sculpture lie within an hour's drive of Forte dei Marmi, and that very nearly all of these are carvings in marble or stone. Past and present pull, therefore, in the same direction; and it seems to me that pieces like the *Knife-edge Sculpture* of 1962 or the *Divided Head* of 1963 are really stone carvings that just happen to have been simulated in plaster and cast in bronze. Nearer to the art of the master-mason than to that of the bronze-founder, they augur a new phase in Moore's work; and that phase was carried forward in the piece known as *The Archer* (1964–5) which underwent a number of metamorphoses but is likewise in essentials an idea-for-stone. By this I mean that the forms are smooth, precise, and regular: an unbroken line leads from one to another. There are no hidden areas, no points at which the eye is led so far and no farther. Nor is there the pull to and fro between inner and outer surfaces which marks the big bronze two- and three-piece sculptures: in fact, there *are* no inner surfaces. *The Archer* is the antithesis of all the pierced pieces which Moore had been making for close on thirty years. And, for all its huge bulk (the big bronze version is almost eleven feet high), it gives no feeling of heaviness: it has a slow, easy, turning-and-circling movement which suggests that if it cared to it could execute an immensely dignified somersault and land, the right way up, on its two feet: the one broad and flat, the other delicate and pointed.

With the exception of the grim-faced *Locking Piece* of 1962, most of the sculptures of the mid 1960s had something of this quality. They looked as if their basic forms had been decided with hammer and chisel, even if whole group of documentary photographs exist to prove that they were built up with splodges of white plaster on an armature of what looks like cheese-cloth and rough-hewn pencils. Sometimes the delicate

207 and 208 Standing Figure (Knife-edge) *Bronze*
9 ft. 4 in. 1961 Perini-San Francisco Associates, San
Francisco

209 and 210 Knife-edge (two-piece) *Bronze length 28 in.*
1962 *Contemporary Arts Society, London*

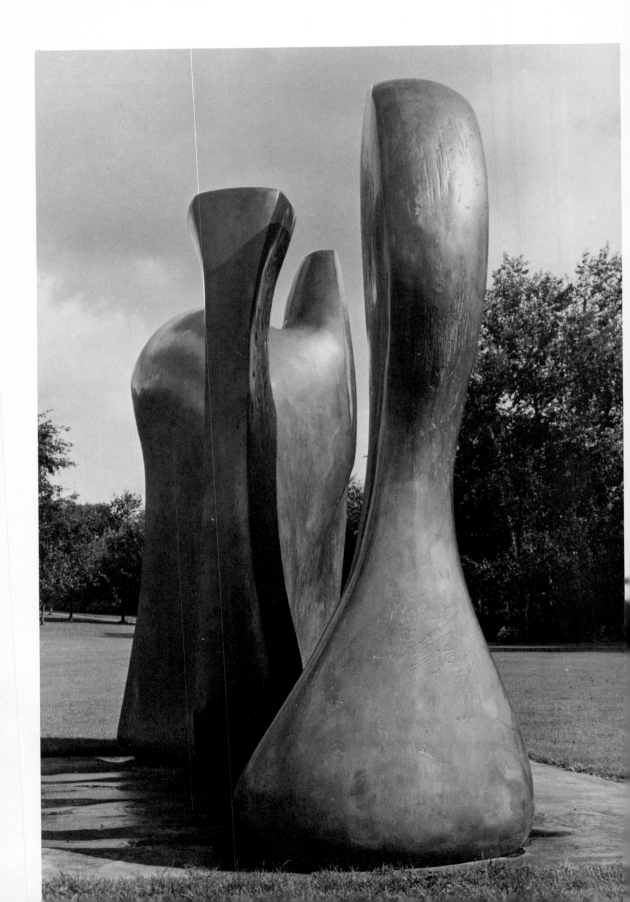

211 Three-way Piece: Archer (in progress) *Plaster*
30½ in. 1964 Artist's Collection

stance of *The Archer* was uppermost: this was the case, for instance, in the *Three-way Piece no. 1: Points* of 1964. At other times, as in the *Divided Head* (1963) and *Moon Head* (1964), bronze was made to do things which made it look like marble, even if in reality neither piece would have been practicable as a carving. Moore had not made a direct carving since the long haul of the elmwood *Reclining Figure*. His is in large degree a tactile imagination; in England he likes above all to keep a dozen ideas going at once, either in the sketch-book or with rapid manipulations in plaster. But in the 1960s the sketch-book serves him less well: the ideas behind a piece like *The Archer* simply cannot be drawn; its spatial existence is altogether complex. So there are no preliminary drawings for *The Archer*: the work exists from start to finish in three dimensions.

At Much Hadham the preliminary explorations go forward in plaster in a curious cup-board-like room heated by an electric fire not much bigger than a jumbo postcard. In Forte dei Marmi, quite other habits were formed. An abundance of fine stone is constantly to hand, and Henraux's often import exotic rarities in the way of business. The tradition of fine hard craftsmanship is immensely alive in the work-shops. Altogether it is stone-country, and stone-manipulator's country, and everything about it represents a challenge to a sculptor who for years communicated above all in stone. Moore began, therefore, to carve in stone all over again, and in the summer of 1967 a group of these new carvings was put on show in London.

They were of many kinds. There was nothing uniform or repetitive about them. *Three Rings* was what it sounds like: a meaningful arrange-ment of three designs in Rose Aurora marble for a ring for Mary Moore. *Two Forms* was in the great succession of Moore's erotic sculptures: a mating-dance momentarily arrested. *Upright Form (Knife-edge)* (pl. 224) and the white marble *Reclining Form* (pl. 225) were late variants of themes which had obsessed Moore for forty years; but they were variants of a particularly subtle and purified sort, in which nothing was left to the happy accidents of casting and the

212 The Archer *Bronze 10 ft. 8 in. 1964–5 Nathan Phillips Square, Toronto*

213 Locking Piece Sculpture (working model) *Bronze*
42 in. 1962 Lehmbruck Museum, Duisburg

214 Working Model, Locking Piece Sculpture *Bronze*
42 in. 1962 Lehmbruck Museum, Duisburg

piece worked continuously throughout 360 degrees. Nor was it only the white radiance of the material which gave the pieces their immaterial look. The *Reclining Figure* seemed, for instance, barely to rest on the ground. They were pieces, also, which resisted interpretation : no one could say, 'These are about survival', as they could of the big two- and three-piece bronzes. The unconscious had kept its rights intact.

An exception to this was the white marble *Torso* (pl. 227). This was as near as Moore had come for twenty years to a straight naturalistic carving. When one thinks of the metaphors for strenuosity with which Moore has so often concerned himself, there is something positively angelic about the ease, the delicacy, and the unerring judgement which went into this study of the human female back. (There is also, of course, an unconcealed sexual scrutiny from which the angels are traditionally exempt.)

Common to all these pieces was a fine-drawn, uninflated quality. Everything lay under the hand. We were back to the proto-Moore of the late 1920s and early 1930s, for whom a sculpture was something that could be spanned by a man's arms. Working close in to the stone, Moore could allow himself a degree of finesse that is not possible in bronze.

Many of the pieces had, also, an open, relaxed quality : they were not at all 'busy'. This came out again, and even more strongly, in the large *Double Oval* which he prepared in plaster at Much Hadham in the spring of 1967. Intended for the Chase Manhattan Bank in New York, this had a beautiful, slow, even pulse. It was, moreover, the first of Moore's major pieces which was expressly designed to be walked through. There were none of the secret, undersized tunnels which, in earlier pieces, could trap an intruder : a smiling openness took their place. Moore was, once again, on the move.

All this came at a time of some difficulty for Moore's reputation. Injustice always results if an artist gets more talked about than looked at. This has been Moore's fate with older people for ten years or more, and it has also been his fate with younger people. Older people still

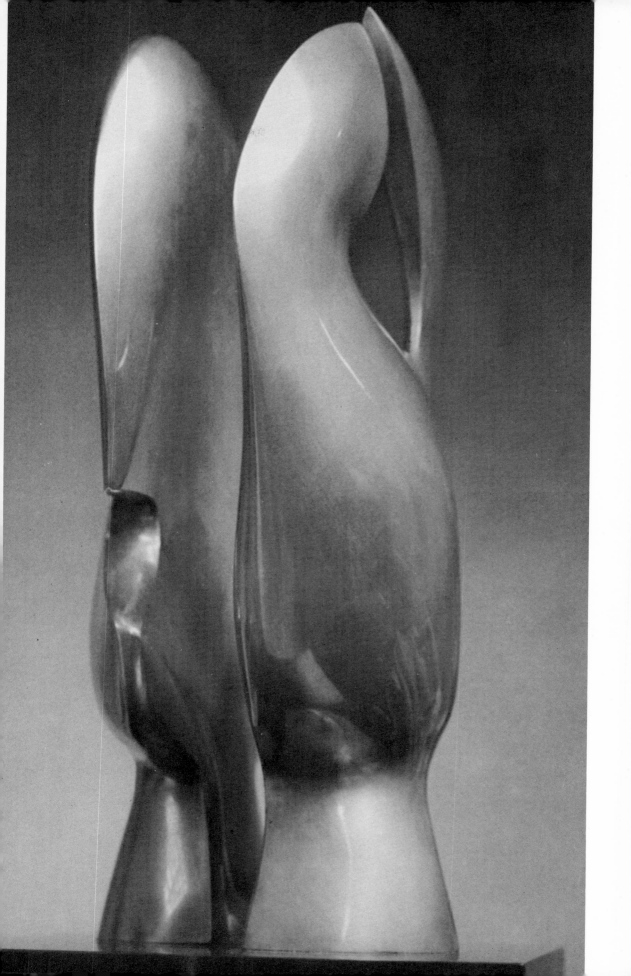

217 Head (divided) *Bronze 13¾ in.* 1963 *Kunsthaus, Zürich*

218 and 219 Moon Head *Bronze 22½ in.* 1964 *Private Collection*

220 and 221 Three Rings *Rosa Aurora marble length 39½ in. 1966 Gordon Bunshaft, New York*

think it rather daring to 'accept' Henry Moore; younger people consider that the repudiation of Moore is a part of growing up, and a part on no account to be omitted. Meanwhile the work – which is what really matters – is not looked at.

There is, of course, a great deal of it. It is almost as difficult to get a grasp of Moore's work, in its totality, as it is to get a grasp of Rodin's. Moore has his anthology pieces, the way Britten has his 'Young Person's Guide' and Auden has 'Out on the lawn I lie in bed': too often, acquaintance with these does duty for a more comprehensive understanding. Criticism of Moore tends to be reverential on the one hand, vituperative on the other. People who have grown up, and grown old, with his work incline to identify with it to such an extent that an attack upon Moore is an attack upon themselves. For young people Moore is, by contrast, a fabled obstruction: if only he and his reputation could be got out of the way! Moore, in this context, is to art what Churchill was to public affairs: the big figure who divides the generations as Moses divided the Red Sea.

This being so, it is not surprising that there should have come into existence a school of sculpture which presents, in effect, a reversed image of everything that Moore has striven for. That sculpture is, broadly speaking, spare, non-allusive, metallic, often brightly coloured, and in intention absolutely distinct from everything that sculpture has meant to earlier generations. This is not the place to discuss to what extent the new sculpture has succeeded in its aims, though it is legitimate to say that older people are often as blind to the merits of Caro and his colleagues as younger people are blind to the merits of Moore. What matters here is the extent to which the history of British sculpture has been shaped by the necessity of finding an alternative to Moore.

I myself find this all the more natural in that Moore himself has so often been affected by that necessity. It will by now, I hope, be clear that there are many Moores, and that some of them are as much antitheses as alternatives. Between the architecture of disquiet and the architecture of consolation there is, for instance, an obvious

222 and 223 Two Forms *Red Soraya Travertine marble*
59 in. 1966 *Artist's Collection*

polarity: and one which Moore has taken care to preserve. Moore has played continually on the great primary oppositions: horizontal/vertical, open/shut, hollow/solid, animal/mineral, tough/tender, passive/active. He has drawn upon a vast range of secondary allusion, much of it ambiguous; but he has never tried to smother the extremes of his nature. Each has been given its turn: tough and tender have equal rights.

Every reader of art literature is wary of the great crashing 'definitive judgement'. Huge claims do not impress posterity, any more than the lifelong resident in the Hôtel des Grands Hommes is necessarily material for the Pantheon. We none of us know to what extent we are the captives of our environment. In particular, we cannot be sure to what extent our responses are to universal qualities, and to what extent they relate to particular and ephemeral needs. The bigger the achievement, the more mysterious the forces involved: the relationship between Cézanne and analytical cubism is, for instance, a long way from its final codification.

Edmund Wilson once said that 'No two people read the same book', and he might equally well have said that no one person reads the same book twice: there is a continual readjustment, not only between different people and 'the same book', but among the elements within any one person which respond to that book. *Middlemarch* is not the same at fifty as it was at eighteen, and this is all the more true of recent works of art with which one has been associated for the whole of one's adult life.

And there is, finally, the question of under- and over-exposure. All successful artists have to cope with this today. Before 1939 it was not so: it was possible, for instance, for Picasso's *Demoiselles d'Avignon* to be finished in 1907 and first put on show thirty years later. Brancusi, likewise, was able to work away with minimal interference from the outer world. Bonnard's studio was full of marvellous canvases which it never occurred to him to publicize. The fatuity of public-relations procedures played no part in serious art-life. It was possible, equally, for an artist like Henri Laurens to live and die in

224 Upright Form (Knife-edge) *White marble 26 in.*
1966 *Marlborough Fine Art, London*

225 Reclining Form *White marble length 43 in.* 1966
Marlborough Fine Art, London

228

226 Two Forms *White marble 18 in. 1963–6 Marlborough Fine Art, London*

227 Torso *White marble 31 in. 1966 Marlborough Fine Art, London*

near-poverty. But, on balance, European art-life was the better for the atmosphere of near-secrecy in which the bigger painters and sculptors went about their work, just as it was the better for the fact that ambassadorial duties were left to ambassadors and the artist was not paraded round Europe under official auspices one year and left for dead the next.

Moore has lived through both periods. He has been in Paris, for instance, as an all-but-anonymous visitor who had to count every centime; and he has been there as the fêted ornament of a series of governmental occasions. When things got to the point at which he could hardly go to the theatre without being followed by a camera-team and a *New Yorker* profile-writer, some people thought that the old, ruminative, and private Moore had gone down in a welter of promotional devices. These were conditions in which it would be very easy for an artist to turn into a one-man souvenir-shop. I myself abhor the practice of casting early Moore carvings in bronze. I also believe that there is an ideal scale for every sculptural idea

and that the practice of marketing larger or smaller replicas of any given idea is in the long run injurious to an artist. A lesser man could have been completely swamped by the adulation which has lately surrounded Moore: and that adulation has provoked, in others, feelings as petty as they are malignant.

With age the senior artist does, of course, inspire a kind of collective involvement which has nothing to do with the quality of his current work. When Voltaire's *Irène* was put on in Paris in 1778, and Voltaire himself went to see it, the plaudits were not for the play but for all that Voltaire had meant to his century. It could be the same with Henry Moore; but it isn't. The *Reclining Figure* and the white *Torso* of 1966 have somehow got clear of adulation. They have an element of unhurrying privacy which reminds us of the days when Moore didn't know where the next bit of stone was coming from. They stand for the quintessential Moore: not the 'seventy-year-old smiling public man' of whom Yeats might have written, but the one who has lived all his life a private adventure.

228 Double Oval *Rosa Aurora marble height 24 in.*
1966 *Marlborough Fine Art, London*

229 Double Oval (in shelter) *Plaster approx. 14 ft.* 1967 *Artist's Collection*

There are other Moores, as everyone knows: and, in particular, there is the Moore who more than once became the keeper of Everyman's conscience. He did this in the Shelter drawings, and he did it when in 1945 the idea of a stable family life re-entered the realm of practicality, and he did it in the *Atom Piece*. He also did it, indirectly, in the late Reclining Figures which suggest that there is, after all, an alternative to pettiness and self-destruction. In all these, the element of public service is somewhere latent: this is not a fashionable impulse, in matters of art, and it is one that usually leads only to rhetorical commonplace. But there is in Henry Moore a broad streak of the nineteenth-century radical, and this has not been at all contaminated by two decades of worldly success. Art for him is a single-handed matter, but it does not exclude the generous meaningful gesture which reminds us that things can be changed for the better and that it is our duty to bring that about.

But if a certain dogged optimism is the mark of Moore's activity on the public front, quite other qualities distinguish the Moore who has dived over and over again below the level of conscious awareness. It is by his readiness to let the demons loose that we recognize this Moore: less metaphorically, we realize that in the mid 1930s, long before the imagery of the 'divided self' was formulated by R. D. Laing, Moore was probing the extent to which an individual personality could be divided, and split off, and set against itself, and yet retain its identity. On this private Moore, much work has still to be done: in the light, above all, of the revised concept of the unconscious which was pioneered by Anton Ehrenzweig in his *The Hidden Order of Art*. Ehrenzweig looked to Moore primarily for his evocations of the 'Great Mother'; later students may prefer to study other and more cryptic aspects of Moore's work. The private Moore has kept his secrets: their deciphering must wait for another time, and another man, and a different book.